Austin K. Graff

111 Places for Kids in Washington, DC That You Must Not Miss

Photographs by Cynthia Schiavetto Staliunas

emons:

To Addy, may we always explore together

Bibliographical information of the Deutsche Nationalbibliothek
The Deutsche Nationalbibliothek lists this publication in the Deutsche Nationalbibliografie; detailed bibliographical data are available on the internet at http://dnb.d-nb.de.

Cäcilienstraße 48, 50667 Köln
info@emons-verlag.de

Layout: Editorial Design & Artdirection, Conny Laue, based on a design by Lübbeke | Naumann | Thoben
Maps: altancicek.design, www.altancicek.de
Basic cartographical information from Openstreetmap, © OpenStreetMap-Mitwirkende, OdbL
Edited by Karen E. Seiger
Printing and binding: sourc-e GmbH
Printed in Europe 2025
ISBN 978-3-7408-2428-0

Did you enjoy this guidebook? Would you like to see more?
Join us in uncovering new places around the world on:
www.111places.com

FOREWORD

For me, my family, and more than 700,000 others, Washington, DC is home. Yes, it's the nation's capital, and millions visit from around the world to snap a photo in front of The White House or go on a US Capitol tour. But there's more to DC than politics and power. It's where children go to school, families shop for groceries, and friends gather at restaurants. With this book as your guide, my deepest hope is that you'll see the city beyond the headlines, a place where a diverse group of people live, some for many generations.

Raising my daughter here turns the city into a playground. I taught her the alphabet by exploring every neighborhood – A is for Anacostia, B is for Brookland, and so on. Iconic buildings melt into our daily life. Every Monday, my family and close friends meet at a woman-owned taco shop. Afterwards, we walk four blocks to play hide-n-seek on the Capitol grounds, which doubles as the country's largest arboretum. I'm usually the one to count as my daughter and friends hide behind trees and bushes.

While you visit DC's museums, look for hidden nooks that are just for kids. When she was a baby, my daughter crawled into a tipi at the National Museum of the American Indian's imagiNATIONS Activity Center. When she was a toddler, she played "chef" at a replica of Julia Child's kitchen on the ground floor of the National Museum of American History. These museums don't just tell stories about our nation – they hold memories for my family and many others.

This book is your guide to popular sites, but it also invites you to explore Washington, DC's many neighborhoods, all of which are steeped in local history. Dance to go-go music, the city's official music, at the Go-Go Museum & Café in Anacostia, one of the oldest neighborhoods here and a center for Black culture.

So start exploring and go find the real city filled with real people and many adventures!

111 PLACES

Lifting
LIMB
Jokes

1_AIR AND SPACE MUSEUM

An X-Wing Starfighter amidst real spacecraft

Star Wars fans, this one's for you. The Smithsonian's Air and Space Museum has a real X-Wing Starfighter from the movie *Star Wars: The Rise of Skywalker* (2019). Often in films, the props are kept simple. Not this X-Wing Starfighter. It's fully built out with 37-foot wings and a model of R2D2 sitting in the cockpit! It's hanging from the ceiling just outside the Albert Einstein Planetarium, so it's easy to miss if you don't look up.

cool

Since the Air and Space Museum opened in 1976, its goal has been to reimagine flight. The *Star Wars* X-Wing Starfighter does just that. Lucasfilm created a world in galaxies far, far away and imagined how flight might work. The X-Wing Starfighter is named after the shape its wings make when it's in the attack position often seen in *Star Wars* movies. To make it realistic, the designers created the spacecraft with dents and nicks as if it was really in a battle and not just part of a movie set.

You'll want to take your time to explore the whole museum. While you remember *Star Wars*, your parents may be excited to see the studio model of the USS *Enterprise* from *Star Trek.* You can also see the Wright Brothers' very first airplane and the spacesuit worn by Neil Armstrong, the first person to walk on the moon in 1969. Step inside a real airplane or try on astronaut gloves at one of the hands-on Discovery Stations throughout the museum. Don't forget about the planetarium, where you can pretend you're flying through space. And always look up to see all kinds of planes.

Address 600 Independence Avenue SW, Washington, DC 20560, +1 (202) 633-2214, www.airandspace.si.edu/visit/museum-dc // **Getting there** Metro to L'Enfant Plaza (Blue, Green, Orange, Silver, Yellow Lines) // **Hours** Daily 10am–5:30pm // **Ages** 2+

TIP: The nearby National Museum of African Art exhibits traditional and modern African art.

2_ALBERT EINSTEIN MEMORIAL

Get close to a famous physicist

DC is filled with many statues, but the Albert Einstein Memorial is only one you're allowed to climb on. The oversized statue of the world's most famous physicist lounges on some steps outside the National Academy of Sciences. Climb onto his lap, and rub his nose for good luck if you're tall enough. In fact, so many people rub the nose of the 12-foot-tall, bronze Einstein statue that it's much shinier than the rest of him.

You may know Einstein for his breakthroughs in physics. He came up with something called the theory of relativity. One of the coolest things about this theory is Einstein's prediction about the existence of black holes, which are dark holes in space that suck in anything in their paths due to their extremely strong forces of gravity.

Most people know of Albert Einstein, but most don't know that he didn't love wearing socks. That's why he's wearing only sandals in his 3.5-ton statue. Another exciting secret is the echo you hear when you face the statue. Down at your feet is a star map of the skies when the Albert Einstein Memorial was dedicated on April 22, 1979.

TIP: Another sandal-wearing statue is that of Mahatma Gandhi in front of the Embassy of India.

Despite Einstein's fame and prestige, he was a modest man, and his statue is wearing casual clothes. The sculptor Robert Berk created the statue from real sketches he made of Einstein in 1953, when the professor was 74 years old. He also created a bust from the sketches, which you can see inside the National Academy of Sciences. You'll find it in the Great Hall, one of the most beautiful rooms in the city.

Address 2101 Constitution Avenue NW, Washington, DC 20418, +1 (202) 334-2000, www.nasonline.org/about-the-nas/locations/the-einstein-memorial // **Getting there** Metro to Foggy Bottom-GWU (Blue, Orange, Silver Lines) // **Hours** Unrestricted // **Ages** 2+

3_ALPHABET ANIMALS

Go on an animal scavenger hunt in Capitol Hill

Just blocks away from the famous Capitol Building's dome, you'll find animal sculptures hidden throughout Capitol Hill. A spider weaving a web, narwhals dancing up a light pole, and a penguin watching traffic are just three of around twenty different sculptures that are part of Capitol Hill Arts Workshop's *Capitol Hill Alphabet Animals*.

Created by local artists and hanging on lamp and light posts, *Capitol Hill Alphabet Animals* make a game out of learning the alphabet while exploring DC's street grid system, where streets running east to west begin with letters. So, where E Street meets 5th Street SE is an emu, the second-largest bird in the world and one of the only birds that can't fly. Look for a ladybug sculpture where L and 2nd Streets SE intersect. At K and 4th Streets SE is where – you guessed it – a koala plays on a lamp post.

TIP: See more alphabet animal sculptures along Connecticut Avenue NW between the National Zoo and Cleveland Park.

There are things to learn from many of the sculptures. Find the honeybee and think about how important bees are for our ecosystem. Bees help pollinate the Earth, help provide medicine, and give us delicious honey. The wood thrush, DC's official bird with a similar frame to a robin, makes an appearance too.

Within the sculpture collection are a few especially fun animals. Where A and 7th Streets SE meet are two sculptures of an ant and an anteater. And don't miss the Capitalsaurus chasing a Falcarius at F and 1st Streets SE, the exact spot where bones of DC's official dinosaur were found in 1898. You'll even find a sign that reads "Capitalsaurus Court."

Address 545 7th Street SE, Washington, DC 20003, www.chaw.org/projects // Getting there Metro to Eastern Market (Blue, Orange, Silver Lines) // Hours Unrestricted // Ages 2+

4_ART MUSEUM OF THE AMERICAS

We share the same hemisphere

Latin America, our southern neighbor, is a region of natural beauty, with its lush jungles, exotic birds, and impressive waterfalls. It's a place of 21 beautiful and diverse countries. One of the best places to learn about this region is at the Art Museum of the Americas Sculpture Garden, part of the Organization of American States (OAS), where leaders in the Western Hemisphere gather. With a clear view of the Washington Monument, it's easily overlooked, but do go see it.

The Art Museum of the Americas is the country's first museum dedicated to modern and contemporary art from Latin America and the Caribbean. It was a gift to the US in 1976 in honor of the country's 200th birthday. As temporary exhibits rotated through, select pieces were pulled to create a permanent sculpture garden. Today, dozens of sculptures and statues teach you about all the region's countries and cultures.

Find *September*, a tall, see-through sculpture of a woman by Marta Minujín from Argentina. The woman depicted is in a nurturing pose to symbolize spring, the start of something new. Why is it called *September* if it honors spring? It's because when it's autumn in North America, it's spring in the Southern Hemisphere. Also spend time in the Garden of Poets and read about writers from places like Peru and Argentina. A life-sized sculpture of Peruvian poet César Vallejo sits on a bench next to a Little Free Library that's sometimes filled with books of his writings. Snap a photo on the bench next to him.

Address 201 18th Street NW, Washington, DC 20006, +1 (202) 370-0147, www.museum.oas.org, artmus@oas.org // Getting there Metro to McPherson Square (Blue, Orange, Silver Lines) // Hours Museum: Tue–Sun 9:30am–1pm & 1:30–5pm; Sculpture Garden: unrestricted // Ages 3+

TIP: Feed the ducks at nearby Constitution Gardens along the National Mall.

5_ARTECHOUSE

Play with technology and art

Artechouse isn't a typical art gallery. In fact, there isn't a single painting or sculpture here. Instead, it's a gallery of light and technology. Among the first of its kind in the world, Artechouse projects artists' work onto giant walls, creating a light show that leaves you in awe.

You'll walk down several flights of stairs until you reach a big, black door. Open it and follow the light, which will take you to a large room, where works of art are beamed onto every wall and even the floor beneath your feet. Bean bags are provided, or you can just plop down on the floor to take in the light show around you. Blue, purple, yellow, green – the colors dance to synchronized music. It's magical.

Every year, several exhibits rotate through Artechouse. Usually during the Cherry Blossom Festival in the springtime, you can come and see a beautiful, cherry blossom-themed show here, with pink and white flowers dancing on every surface. Some of them even respond to your own movements. Lift up your arms, and you'll see the blossoms start dancing faster.

Three additional rooms at Artechouse host technology-driven art exhibits, including interactive experiences that make learning fun. One past exhibit focused on the ocean as its theme. It included a video game-like station, where you could make a deep-sea creature swim up the water as you learned facts about it. If you download the Artechouse app, it will take you on a scavenger hunt during your visit. And have fun at the coloring stations.

Address 1238 Maryland Avenue SW, Washington, DC 20024, www.artechouse.com, dc@artechouse.com // **Getting there** Metro to L'Enfant Plaza (Blue, Green, Orange, Silver, Yellow Lines) // **Hours** Daily 10am–10pm // **Ages** 2+

TIP: Walk to nearby Maryland Avenue Linear Park for a great view of the Washington Monument.

6_BARRY FARM AQUATIC CENTER

Splash year round

Four seasons are part of Washington, DC's rhythms. When the humidity and heat descend on the city during the summer, you'll want to know the best pools. When winter comes and the cold has you dreaming of the beach, indoor pools become key. Luckily, the Barry Farm Aquatic Center is a place in the city where you can swim any season of the year.

Step inside, and you'll see that the pool is divided equally between a lap pool for adults and an area for young swimmers. Kids will love the spigots spouting water into the air and buckets filling up with water before pouring it on the heads of whoever is below. There's also a water slide with several twists and turns. If you need a life vest for extra measure, there's a rack full of them.

Barry Farm Aquatic Center is part of a large recreation center with outdoor fields, a space-themed playground, murals, a game room, and more. It's along Sumner Road, named after Massachusetts Senator Charles Sumner, who was a leading voice in abolishing slavery in the 19th century.

In fact, many roads near Barry Farm are named after Civil War Union generals, abolitionists, and other voices in the fight to end slavery in the United States. This aquatic center sits in a neighborhood settled shortly after the end of the Civil War by people who were once enslaved. The war was fought for their freedom so they could play freely outside, just like the kids today. As you splash in the pool, remember the price of freedom many paid so all can be free in this country.

Address 1230 Sumner Road SE, Washington, DC 20020, +1 (202) 442-5420, dpr.dc.gov/page/barry-farm-aquatic-center, dpr@dc.gov // **Getting there** Metro to Anacostia (Green Line) // **Hours** Mon–Fri 6am–9pm, Sat & Sun 10am–5pm // **Ages** 2+

TIP: Visit Deanwood Aquatic Center for more waterslides.

7_BEATLES' FIRST US CONCERT

Rock out in an old concert space

If you don't know who The Beatles are, ask your parents. With top songs like "Hey Jude" and "A Day in the Life," they were, and in many ways still are, one of the world's most famous bands. A band born in the United Kingdom, The Beatles' first concert in the United States wasn't in New York City or Los Angeles. It happened in Washington, DC in 1964.

After appearing on a TV show in New York City, The Beatles took a train, through a snowstorm, to DC to play at the Washington Coliseum, just steps away from Union Station, in front of over 8,000 fans. The concert lasted 35 minutes, and the Beatles played 12 songs to an audience that could barely hear the lyrics due to the venue's poor acoustics. Ask any Washingtonian who was there, including a young Al Gore, who later became Vice President, and they will recall many memories of the iconic evening. The stage was in the middle of the coliseum, meaning the band only faced a quarter of the audience. The Beatles turned their equipment around throughout the concert so every fan could see their faces.

The Washington Coliseum building is still around, but it's now an REI store where you can pick up camping gear, bikes, and more kits for the outdoors. Walk inside and look for the large concrete columns with posters honoring The Beatles' first US concert. Outside the large building along Third Street NE is a restored call box (once used to call the police and fire department before houses had phones) with art depicting The Beatles' four famous members.

Address 201 M Street NE, Washington, DC 2000, +1 (202) 543-2040, www.rei.com/stores/washington-dc // Getting there Metro to NoMa-Gallaudet U (Red Line) // Hours Daily 10am–9pm // Ages 5+

TIP: Find a vertical playground at the nearby Swampoodle Dog Park & Playground.

8_BECAUSE SCIENCE

Make your own slime or lava lamp

The phrase "Science is for everyone" is featured on the rainbow mural at the entryway to Because Science, a woman-owned store that sells science-themed toys, gifts, and art. After a few minutes inside this store, you'll want to be a scientist when you grow up.

Because Science's shelves are filled with everything from toys, like atom-shaped Squishmallows and model solar systems, to kits to make your own root beer. Browse the book corner to find joke books about the human body and children's books about famous people like Jane Goodall, who spent her entire life studying and caring for chimpanzees. Every item in the store has a connection to science. Even the greeting cards are about science: they're embedded with seeds, and you can plant them to grow flowers and herbs in your garden.

This wonderful store makes a number of their own products, too, like the stickers of chemistry beakers. One wall showcases art made from circuit boards, including a DC flag and even earrings made from the electronic parts. Circuit boards are the parts that are used in electronic devices to protect you from getting a shock.

The back of the shop is where the magic happens. This is where they keep a lab to make the circuit board art. In fact, you can sign up for a class to make your own art out of circuit boards. Staff will teach you how to safely take apart an electronic device. Then you can make your own masterpiece using its pieces to take home. Other workshops teach you how to make your own slime or lava lamp.

Address 1759 Columbia Road NW, Washington, DC 20009, +1 (202) 248-1366, www.becausesciencedc.com, info@becausesciencedc.com // **Getting there** Metro to Woodley Park-Zoo/Adams Morgan (Red Line) // **Hours** Sun–Thu noon–6pm, Fri & Sat 11am–7pm // **Ages** 4+

TIP: Kalorama Park is nearby, with two playgrounds and green space for picnics.

9_BEN'S CHILI BOWL

Eat a famous half-smoke

A half-smoke is an iconic food from DC, like a hotdog, but larger, a little spicier, and made with half pork and half beef. The most famous place to order one is Ben's Chili Bowl. Order a plain or have it the traditional way with mustard, onions, and chili.

The story behind Ben's Chili Bowl is inspiring. Just a few weeks after getting married in 1958, Ben and Virginia Ali opened the restaurant inside an old movie theater, making it one of DC's longest-standing restaurants. Over the years, they have served millions of half-smokes to locals and tourists, including many important people. When Martin Luther King Jr. gave his famous "I Have A Dream" speech during the 1963 March on Washington, the Alis helped feed the crowd.

And they will feed you. On the menu, you'll see more than their famous half-smoke. Chili is king here. It comes on the half-smoke, by itself in a cup, or on top of cheese fries. Or you can get loaded chili fries with all the fixings like sour cream and tomatoes. For dessert, choose a milkshake from eight flavors. Don't leave without tasting the banana pudding. In the back is an old-school jukebox and countless photos of famous patrons. Barack Obama is part of the gallery.

While you're there, ask for Virginia Ali, called "Mama" by everyone. Almost 100 years old, Virginia often greets her customers. She believes in treating everyone with kindness, and she loves seeing families eat her famous half-smokes. Kids can run around the back room in between sips of milkshakes.

Address 1213 U Street NW, Washington, DC 20009, +1 (202) 667-0909, www.benschilibowl.com, hello@benschilibowl.com // **Getting there** Metro to U Street/African-American Civil War Memorial/Cardozo (Green & Yellow Lines) // **Hours** Sun–Thu 11am–11pm, Fri & Sat 11am–4am // **Ages** 4+

TIP: Walk down the next-door alley to see murals of Black icons.

10_BETHUNE MEMORIAL

Honoring a Black hero

One of the few statues that depict children in Washington, DC is part of the Mary McLeod Bethune Memorial in Lincoln Park. The memorial includes statues of two children, a boy and girl, playing with Mary McLeod Bethune, a civil rights activist and educator. This memorial is an important one. Designed by sculptor Robert Berks, it went up in 1974 on the 99th anniversary of Bethune's birthday. It was the first statue in DC honoring a woman and a Black hero on federal land.

In case you haven't learned about Mary McLeod Bethune in your history class yet, here's her story. The daughter of formerly enslaved parents, Bethune had a vision to help create a country where everyone is treated equally regardless of the color of their skin. She started several organizations to champion civil rights for the Black community, created a school for Black students, and served as an advisor to President Franklin D. Roosevelt. She was an inspiration to many.

TIP: Play on the two enclosed playgrounds in Lincoln Park.

When her memorial was erected, it joined another statue within Lincoln Park of Abraham Lincoln freeing an enslaved man. This statue used to face the US Capitol but was rotated toward the Mary McLeod Bethune Memorial. It would be rude for Lincoln to turn his back on a woman, especially one of such significance.

The best way to honor and celebrate Mary McLeod Bethune is on her birthday every year on July 10, when the National Park Service throws a party for her. There's face painting, story time, and even sweet potato pie.

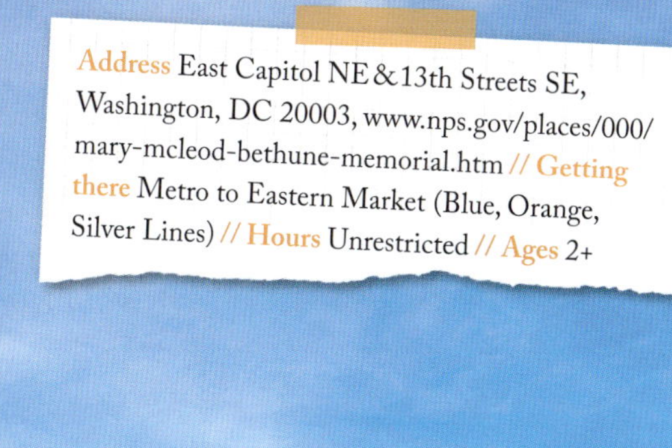

Address East Capitol NE & 13th Streets SE, Washington, DC 20003, www.nps.gov/places/000/mary-mcleod-bethune-memorial.htm // **Getting there** Metro to Eastern Market (Blue, Orange, Silver Lines) // **Hours** Unrestricted // **Ages** 2+

11_THE BIG CHAIR

It's an eye-popping sight

In the middle of historic Anacostia along a busy street is a very, very big chair. It's actually called The Big Chair, and it's so big that you can't even climb it. The legs are taller than any person. Even a basketball player like DC native Kevin Durant couldn't reach, and he's 6 feet 1 inches.

How did this giant chair get here? It started out as a publicity stunt for Curtis Brothers Furniture, a furniture company that used to be inside a large building near The Big Chair. To help attract customers, they installed The Big Chair. Within its first year, the furniture company built a glass house on top and paid a model to live in it for the summer. People would travel to see the glass house. Weird, right?

Through the 1968 riots and gentrification, The Big Chair still stood. Over the years, though, its joints broke because of the wind across the nearby Anacostia River. After many repairs, it was taken down, which caused an uproar. Neighbors loved The Big Chair so much that they replaced it with an aluminum one in 2006 to withstand the test of time.

It's no longer considered the world's largest chair, but it holds many neighborhood stories. Santa Claus used to sit on the chair and wave to passersby every December. It's respected so much that no one tags it with spray paint or tries to destroy it. It's considered a symbol of hope to the community. Everyone in Anacostia knows The Big Chair, and you better remember its proper name. You must call it "The Big Chair," never just "Big Chair."

TIP: The Anacostia Arts Center regularly hosts free jazz events.

Address 1001-1199 V Street SE, Washington, DC 20020, www.curtisinvestments.com/about-curtis/the-big-chair // **Getting there** Metro to Anacostia (Green Line) // **Hours** Unrestricted // **Ages** 2+

12_BLUE ROOSTER

A giant rooftop statue

If you're walking along the famous Pennsylvania Avenue NW, look up. You may notice a giant, blue rooster on the rooftop of the National Gallery of Art (National Gallery), an art museum with the only painting by Leonardo Da Vinci in the Americas. Go inside to see the blue rooster up close. After all, the museum is free and open every day.

The National Gallery has two buildings, so make sure you go into the East Building. Take the elevator to the rooftop to find the large blue rooster. The statue is named *Hahn/Cock*. A German artist named Katharina Fritsch created the statue for a public square in London. Many months later, *Hahn/Cock* crossed the ocean to Washington, DC. When the whimsical statue made its temporary home on the National Gallery of Art's rooftop in 2016, it became a popular sight. Towering 14 feet tall, it makes kids squeal with delight when they see it.

Today, *Hahn/Cock* is a permanent piece in the National Gallery, and the meaning behind it is inspiring. In old books and tales, roosters often represent strength. To that end, *Hahn/Cock* was given to the National Gallery by the Glenstone Foundation in honor of the resilience of the American people during the Covid-19 pandemic.

TIP: See the grand Bartholdi Fountain by the man who created the Statue of Liberty inside the nearby Bartholdi Gardens.

When you visit, ask a nearby security guard to snap a photo of you in front of the giant rooster. Afterwards, wander around on the rooftop. There's another piece of art popular among kids – giant numbers. Find the number that matches how old you are. Look out across the city for an unexpected view of the US Capitol Building. It's so close, you feel like you can touch it. Don't miss Pennsylvania Avenue NW where Presidential Inauguration Parades happen.

Address 4th Street & Constitution Avenue NW, Washington, DC 20565, +1 (202) 737-4215, www.nga.gov/hahncock, visit@nga.gov // **Getting there** Metro to Archives-Navy Memorial-Penn Quarter (Green & Yellow Lines) // **Hours** Daily 10am–5pm // **Ages** 2+

13_BOUNDARY STONES

Find old monuments

Many people miss the Boundary Stones, the oldest monuments purchased by the United States's government. Hidden in public parks, people's front yards, and forests, the Boundary Stones make for a fun scavenger hunt across the city. Before you go searching, it's important to know why these stones exist.

A long time ago, the US fought the Revolutionary War with Great Britain to become an independent nation in 1776. Once the US won the war, George Washington became the first president. One of the many tasks he had to do was create a capital city. Maryland and Virginia gave land to create what's now Washington, DC. To show everyone the borders of the capital city, large stones were placed. Each stone has the phrase "United States of America" etched into it, the first time the phrase was ever inscribed anywhere.

An interesting fact about Washington, DC is that Virginia took back the land they originally gave to create the capital. So because the city's borders have changed over time, you'll find the Boundary Stones in Virginia, Maryland, and Washington, DC. There were 40 originally, but a few have gone missing over the years. A man named Stephen Powers keeps track of where you can find each one. If you crack the mystery of where the missing ones went, let him know!

When you find one, you'll notice a fence around it protecting it from going missing. These stones have been in the ground since the 1700s, which means they witnessed some major events like the Civil War and the Moon Landing. It's a miracle most are still in the ground!

TIP: Find the statue of Andrew Jackson, the seventh president, in Lafayette Square.

Address Various locations, www.boundarystones.org, contact@boundarystones.org // **Getting there** See website for locations // **Hours** Unrestricted // **Ages** 3+

TOP SECRET

14_BUREAU OF ENGRAVING & PRINTING

This is how your paper money is made

Did you know that Martha Washington appeared on a one-dollar bill before her husband George Washington? You can learn that, and more, at the US Bureau of Engraving & Printing (BEP), one of two places in the entire country that prints paper money. Free tours are offered every weekday to watch millions of dollars printed before your eyes, but it's top secret. Phones and cameras aren't allowed on the tour.

After passing security, you'll enter a lobby with an exhibit about the Bureau's history. The grand building along the National Mall opened in 1914 and has printed paper every single day since then. Ever wonder what one million dollars looks like? There's a stack of $1,000,000 in 10-dollar bills in a glass case in the lobby!

After a brief video, a guide will walk you through the secure facilities, explaining how paper money is made. You'll learn interesting facts – like paper money is made of more cloth than paper. That's why it can go through the laundry without tearing. You'll wave to the men and women who print the money. Many are war veterans and all have the highest security clearances. Spot the sign that reads, "We make money the old fashioned way, we print it."

TIP: Nearby is the Floral Library, a seasonal garden with tulips.

The tour ends inside the visitor center and gift shop, where you'll see old dollar bills. You'll see a $1,000 note and even a $10,000 bill! Before you leave, make sure you see how tall you are in $100 bills.

Address 301 14th Street SW, Washington, DC 20250, +1 (202) 874-2330, www.bep.gov/visitor-centers // Getting there Metro to Smithsonian (Blue, Orange, Silver Lines) // Hours Daily, see website for seasonal hours // Ages 6+

DEPARTMENT OF THE TREASURY
BUREAU OF ENGRAVING AND PRINTING
TOUR ENTRANCE
NOTICE

15_CATACOMBS OF DC

Explore an underground world

You can step down inside real catacombs in the Franciscan Monastery of the Holy Land in America. That might sound scary, and it kind of is, but catacombs are interesting and important. In ancient cities like Rome and Paris, catacombs were built as underground cemeteries in tunnels and rooms. But you don't have to go all the way to Europe, because you can explore catacombs right here in DC. These passageways are dark and a little creepy, but they are worth the intrigue.

These catacombs are special. They are in an area called Little Rome, so named because of the many Catholic churches and organizations in the neighborhood. When the monastery was built, gardens, churches, and shrines were created to replicate ones found in Israel and Rome. The catacombs in DC are modeled after the ones in Rome, where the pope lives.

Anyone can visit the Franciscan Monastery catacombs. When you join one of the regular tours, you'll walk down steep stairs into the catacombs. Passing through dimly lit, narrow tunnels, you'll find a few small rooms with paintings on the walls. The early catacombs housed the remains of martyrs, and so do these ones. Do be prepared to visit the mummy of a child, known as Saint Innocent, and the bones of a 2nd-century martyr.

After the tour, spend time in the monastery's vast gardens filled with tulips and roses, depending on the season. Paths lead you to grottos, man-made caves, and replicas of shrines in the Holy Land. Find the portico with "Hail Mary" written in over 150 languages.

Address 1400 Quincy Street NE, Washington, DC 20017, +1 (202) 526-6800, www.myfranciscan.org, mail@myfranciscan.com // **Getting there** Metro to Brookland-CUA (Red Line) // **Hours** Tours: Tue, Wed, Fri & Sat 1pm & 2pm, Sun noon & 1:30pm; Garden: daily 9am–4pm // **Ages** 7+

TIP: Cool off in the splash pad at nearby Turkey Thicket Recreation Center.

16_DC BOULDERING PROJECT

Climb away

Elbow room is hard to come by in DC, which is, after all, only 68 square miles after Virginia took back their land in 1847 (that's a story for another time). Today, it's easy to drive from one end to the other. That's why it was a big deal when the DC Bouldering Project opened the city's first climbing gym inside a massive space that hosts tall walls for climbing, including a 55-foot-long overhang called "The Beast"!

Located in a historic neighborhood called Eckington that had electricity before it was installed in The White House, the DC Bouldering Project is an adventure-filled place for anyone aged four years and older. Go with a guardian, and someone on staff will teach you the basics of climbing. Finding routes and falling with confidence are the two lessons here. After a few minutes, start picking out colorful route markers to determine your path. Then climb away!

Growing together is part of DC Bouldering Project's vision for its climbing community. To grow, falling is required, and it will happen. But you will always fall safely. No matter how good someone is at climbing, falling is part of the sport. So just get up, shake it off, and climb again.

For young climbers, there's a kids' room with smaller climbing walls, basketball hoops, a foosball table, and books. There's even a quiet area for those who need a break from climbing. It's in this room where the DC Bouldering Project hosts birthday parties, day camps, and other kid activities. They make climbing fun!

Address 1611 Eckington Place NE, #150, Washington, DC 20002, +1 (202) 667-2404, www.boulderingproject.com/location/eckington // Getting there Metro to NoMa-Gallaudet U (Red Line) // Hours Mon–Fri 6am–10pm, Sat & Sun 8am–8pm // Ages 4+

TIP: Close by is Alethia Tanner Park, named after the woman who created the first school for free Black children.

17_DINOSAUR POCKET PARK

Where toy dinos play

The smallest kids often find this pocket park first. Low to the ground in the front yard of a rowhouse, blue, green, pink, and yellow toy dinosaurs stand on rocks waiting to be played with – a mere mile from where real dinosaur bones were discovered years ago. It's an example of a movement called "Sidewalk Joy," creating spaces along paths to spread happiness – and a prime example at that.

Raising a little boy in a big city, the creator of this tiny park saw the curiosity in her son's eyes as they explored the streets. Inspired by the idea of spreading joy through sidewalk art, together they built this mini park and decided to fill it with toy dinosaurs. Why toy dinosaurs? Because they are fun, happy, colorful, and inexpensive to keep the park full.

Kids are free to take one of the dinos as a memento. Sometimes neighbors and guests add their own toys to the collection, like a pair of frog statues. On occasion, the park's owner and her son will place a toy dinosaur inside a water balloon and freeze it. Then they cut off the balloon and place the ice in the pocket park. Passersby enjoy watching the ice melt away to reveal the beast inside!

In between the National Mall and the Wharf, the park's street is usually busy with locals and tourists alike walking by. It's easy to miss, but don't. The tiny dinosaurs spark joy and bring a smile to people's faces, the goal of its creator and her son. Take a toy dinosaur as a new friend and travel companion as you explore the nation's capital!

FUN

TIP: Visit another toy dinosaur pocket park at 4419 36th Street NW.

Address 602 7th Street SW, Washington, DC 20024, www.instagram.com/prehistoricpocketpark // **Getting there** Metro to L'Enfant Plaza (Blue, Green, Orange, Silver, Yellow Lines) // **Hours** Unrestricted // **Ages** 2+

W DC Prehistor
Park

18_DRUM CIRCLE AT MERIDIAN HILL

Dance to the rhythms in a park with views

Learn how to play the drums at one of Washington, DC's most carefree events. On Sunday afternoons year-round, drummers and dancers gather on the top level of Meridian Hill/Malcolm X Park near the statue of Joan of Arc. As the hours go by, the crowd gets larger and larger. Adults and kids alike dance, filling the air with joy.

The tradition has roots in the Civil Rights Movement. In the 1960s and 1970s, drummers would gather here and play music as a way to demand that all people be treated equally in the nation. Decades later, the tradition remains.

Kids are welcome guests – and stars – at the drum circle. A dozen or more drummers will allow kids of all ages to take a turn keeping the beat. Experienced drummers help guide your hands on the bongo drum, teaching you the rhythm. If you stumble, don't worry. Any beats add to the music. Sometimes dance circles break out to the beat of the drums. Anyone can jump in the middle and dance any way they like as everyone claps. Any dance, even silly ones, are met with cheering.

TIP: Visit the Mexican Cultural Institute to learn about our neighbor to the south.

As the music lingers, kids enjoy playing near the 13-basin, cascading fountain, one of the longest in the continent. Four statues – the poet *Dante Alighieri*, *Joan of Arc*, the allegorical *Serenity*, and the *James Buchanan Memorial* – make for a fun scavenger hunt. *Joan of Arc*, honoring the patron saint of France and a heroine often considered the savior of France, is the easiest to find. It's also the only statue in DC that features a woman on a horse.

Address 16th Street NW & W Street NW, Washington, DC 20009, +1 (202) 895-6000, www.nps.gov/places/meridian-hill-park.htm // Getting there Metro to Columbia Heights (Green & Yellow Lines) // Hours Daily dawn–dusk // Ages 2+

19_DUPONT UNDERGROUND

Explore an underground world

As you walk around Dupont Circle, you'll find steps that seem to lead to nowhere, but don't be fooled. These steps lead to the Dupont Underground, an old streetcar tunnel. Before cars became common, most people traveled from one end of the city to the other on streetcars that ran on tracks in the roads, sort of like a train. Streetcars aren't as common in the United States any more, but they are in Europe.

Once streetcars had to share the road with these new vehicles called "cars" in the 1940s, traffic became worse and worse. Imagine sitting in the car for a long time stuck behind a streetcar. No one ever wants that. So the city built an underground tunnel for the streetcars to pass along the traffic circle. However, it was short-lived, as the tunnel closed in 1961.

Then came the Cold War. Dupont Underground was turned into a bomb shelter and was stocked with all kinds of supplies to feed up to 3,000 people. Luckily, it was never needed and was later turned into a failed food court. Today, Dupont Underground is a cultural space – and a spooky one at that.

Walk down the steps into an underground art world. You'll see murals that go on for three blocks, one of the longest stretches of public art in DC. Events are often hosted in this unique space, from ballet performances to art exhibits. Every year, there's a Halloween party, and it's one of the best in the city. Scared to go on your own? Don't worry – they host monthly tours of the tunnel for kids and their families.

Address 19 Dupont Circle NW, Washington, DC 20036, www.dupontunderground.org, connect@dupontunderground.org // **Getting there** Metro to Dupont Circle (Red Line) // **Hours** Fri–Sun 11am–5pm; see website for events schedule // **Ages** 3+

TIP: The nearby Tabard Inn is the city's oldest inn, and they serve warm doughnut.

20_EAST POTOMAC MINI GOLF

Play on the oldest mini golf course

On an island in the Potomac River is East Potomac Miniature Golf, the country's oldest miniature golf course. Where else can you hit a golf ball through The White House, US Capitol, and even George Washington's Mount Vernon? Situated next to a full-fledged golf course, the mini golf course is for all ages – no experience needed. Anyone can play!

Surrounded by views of DC's iconic monuments, this miniature golf course offers 18 holes, each with its unique features. Some have ramps you have to conquer, and others have sharp turns to get around. There are even hills for your golf ball to climb if you hit it just right. Kids can play another round for free Mondays through Thursdays. Once you're all done, you can continue the golf fun at the putting area at the East Potomac Golf Course next door.

The mini golf course's history is well preserved, and signs throughout the course share its stories. Read all the signs to learn that the course's brickwork is original. So is the ticket booth from when it first opened in 1931. You'll learn that the mini golf course was once segregated. Protests took place after a group of Black men played on the course in 1941. But the next day, the course was opened for everyone to enjoy regardless of the color of their skin.

If you play with your family, you'll have to be patient in between your turns. To help pass the time, fun music blasts from speakers throughout the course. And stop by the concession stand for ice cream and other yummy snacks and drinks.

Address 972 Ohio Drive SW, Washington, DC 20024, +1 (202) 554-7660, www.playdcgolf.com/the-miniature-golf-course-at-east-potomac-golf-links // **Getting there** Metro to L'Enfant Plaza (Blue, Orange, Silver Lines) // **Hours** Apr–Oct daily 10am–9pm; Nov–Mar daily 10am–7pm; book tee times online // **Ages** 6+

TIP: Walk to the southern tip of Hains Point to see planes landing at Reagan National Airport.
14

21_EXORCIST STAIRS

Run up some very spooky steps

Ask your parents about a famous, very scary movie called *The Exorcist* based on a story of a child from the Washington, DC area. Filmed partly in the city, the movie includes a scene where a character falls down very steep stairs. That staircase is real, and it's in Georgetown.

Start at the bottom of the stairs, where you'll see a plaque honoring the scene in the movie. While you're near the plaque, look up the stairs. It's a daunting sight. First of all, the stairs are old and dark. Secondly, there are 75 steps in total. Take a deep breath and walk up. Or if you dare, run up. Just be careful and hold onto the railing.

When you get about half way up, stop, rest your feet, and turn around. You'll see a view of tall buildings across the Potomac River. That's a neighborhood called Rosslyn in Arlington, Virginia. It sticks out because there aren't many tall buildings in Washington, DC. Some say that's because buildings can't be taller than the US Capitol or the Washington Monument, but that's just a rumor. The real reason is because of the Height of Buildings Act in 1910, which required buildings to be no taller than the width of the adjacent street.

Before these famous stairs were known as the "Exorcist Stairs," locals called them the "Hitchcock Steps" because of their spookiness. Don't be afraid – once you're at the top, you'll see a beautiful view, and there's much to explore in Georgetown. But if you're up for the challenge, head back down. How many times can you go up and down the stairs?

TIP: Decatur Terrace hosts DC's Spanish Steps, inspired by the ones in Rome.

Address 1825 Water Street NW, Washington, DC 20006 // **Getting there** Bus 38B to 33rd & M Streets NW // **Hours** Unrestricted // **Ages** 6+

22_FALA THE SCOTTISH TERRIER

Pet a president's dog

Did you know that every US president had pets in The White House except for three? There's a long history of pets at The White House. Many presidents have had dogs, like Obama's Portuguese Water Dogs Bo and Sunny, and Harding's terrier Laddie Boy. Then there were cats, like Bill Clinton's Socks.

But some presidents, such as Theodore Roosevelt, brought in snakes and guinea pigs. James Madison let his sheep chew The White House lawn. Parrots, horses, and many other animals have lived at The White House. A rumor still remains that John Quincy Adams let an alligator stay in the East Room for a few weeks. And there's one famous president's dog that you can pet today: Fala, President Franklin D. Roosevelt's (FDR) Scottish terrier.

One of the largest memorials along the Tidal Basin, the FDR Memorial honors all four terms the 32nd US president served. (We have him to thank for limiting presidencies to no more than two terms today.) There are many special parts to the memorial, including a statue of Fala. Created by sculptor Neil Estern, it's the only statue of a president's pet in Washington, DC.

Nearby is a grand sculpture of President Roosevelt himself. Estern also sculpted a statue of Eleanor Roosevelt, the only memorial to a First Lady along the National Mall. Another unique aspect is a statue of FDR sitting in a wheelchair. During his presidency, he hid the fact that he'd had polio and could not walk. He's an inspiration to differently abled kids and adults everywhere.

TIP: The nearby Martin Luther King Jr. Memorial is the only one on the National Mall honoring a Black American.

Address 1850 West Basin Drive SW, Washington, DC 20004, +1 (202) 426-6841, www.nps.gov/frde/index.htm // Getting there Metro to Smithsonian (Blue, Orange, Silver Lines) // Hours Unrestricted // Ages 2+

23_ FISHING AT FLETCHER'S COVE

Catch fish at a historic bay

Most US states have an Official Fish, and DC's is the American shad, which is unique to the East Coast. In fact, it's known as "the fish that fed the nation's founders." George and Martha Washington must have enjoyed a big plate of freshly caught American shad!

You can catch American shad yourself at Fletcher's Cove. From February to early summer, fish from the ocean swim up the Potomac River. People come from around the country to catch American shad, hickory shad, flathead catfish, and blue catfish.

You must throw back most of the fish you catch to help preserve their species, but you can keep catfish. Blue catfish are the most populous in the DC area after thousands were released in Virginia in the 1980s. Flathead catfish are invasive, which means they eat native fish like the American and hickory shad. But if you catch a shad, you have to release it back into the water. They are native to the area, and there aren't very many around today because of overfishing and pollution.

Kids can fish with someone aged 16 or older who has a fishing license. It only takes a few minutes to apply for a license online. A tackle shop at Fletcher's Cove sells supplies and snacks, and you can rent a fishing rod from Anacostia Park's Aquatic Resources Education Center for free March through October. Fish along the river or rent a rowboat or canoe at the cove to fish in the open water. You can even rent kayaks and paddleboards from Boating In DC at Fletcher's Cove.

Address 4940 Canal Road NW, Washington, DC 20016, +1 (202) 337-9642, www.nps.gov/choh/planyourvisit/fletchers-cove.htm // **Getting there** Bus D94 to MacArthur Boulevard & U Street NW // **Hours** Daily dawn–dusk // **Ages** 4+

TIP: Nearby is the 19th-century Abner Cloud House, the oldest home along the canal.

24_FOLGER'S PRINTING PRESS

Learn how books were once made

Once upon a time, people made books by hand. Long before computers and printers, books were created on what's called a printing press. To see a replica of an ancient printing press, head to the Folger Shakespeare Library, home to the world's largest collection of Shakespeare's works. It's a fun way to learn about book making!

Steps away from the US Capitol, the Folger Shakespeare Library houses an interactive exhibit to teach you about the life of playwright William Shakespeare. In the center of the main exhibit is a replica of the printing press that printed Shakespeare's first work centuries ago. Often, staff stand nearby to show you how the printing press works. Ink is placed on the typeface and pressed down on big pieces of paper using a big, wooden crank.

You can't touch the replica printing press, but next door is one that you can touch! You can spell as many words and phrases as you like using typefaces nearby. Spell out a favorite Shakespeare quote or use the letters to spell your name. Nearby, you can fold your own book or test your calligraphy skills.

There's a lot to explore inside the Folger Shakespeare Library. Pick up a scavenger hunt packet at the Welcome Desk and follow clues through the galleries to decode messages, solve riddles, and write a poem. A rare book collection includes many recognizable children's books. The upper level has a real Shakespeare theater and a spacious café called Quill & Crumb that sells treats, like hot cocoa and pastries.

TIP: Pick up free art at the nearby Little Free Art Gallery at 313 East Capitol Street SE.

Address 201 East Capitol Street SE, Washington, DC 20003, +1 (202) 544-4600, www.folger.edu // Getting there Metro to Capitol South (Blue, Orange, Silver Lines) // Hours Sun, Tue & Wed 11am–6pm, Fri–Sun 11am–9pm // Ages 3+

25_FORD'S THEATRE

The nation's most infamous theater

One of the country's most famous theaters is Ford's Theatre simply because it's in every US history book. It's the site where President Abraham Lincoln was infamously assassinated in 1865. While most Americans recognize the name, many don't know it's still a working theater. Shows come to its stage throughout the year, including a spring musical for kids and Charles Dickens' *A Christmas Carol* during the holidays.

The actual theater first opened in 1863, but there are three more sites directly related to Ford's Theatre. Attached to the theater is a museum filled with items associated with Lincoln's assassination. You can see the coat he was wearing when he was shot and the pillow placed under his head as he passed away. The museum is interactive and even hosts sensory-friendly experiences where you can touch pieces within the collection.

The second site associated with Ford's Theatre is the Petersen House, the home of the tailor who took Lincoln in the night he was shot. The next morning Lincoln died there. Today, visitors can walk through the house, which is set up exactly how it looked when the president died in 1865.

Connected to the Petersen House is the Education Center, the third piece to Ford's Theatre. It's where special programs are run and is the home to something very unique. Inside its lobby is a three-story tower of books about Abraham Lincoln. With more than 15,000 books about the president, he's the most written-about American. Look up to see hundreds of books spiral into the air.

TIP: Visit the Lincoln Memorial and try to spot the misspelling etched into the north wall.

Address 511 10th Street NW, Washington, DC 20004, +1 (202) 347-4833, www.fords.org // **Getting there** Metro to Metro Center (Blue, Orange, Red, Silver Lines) // **Hours** Daily 9am–5pm // **Ages** 5+

"I love him not because he was perfect,
but because he was not, and yet triumphed."
–W.E.B. DuBois on Lincoln
Leadership Gallery
ABRAHAM LINCOLN
1858
LINCOLN
DARK
The Lincoln Funeral Train
ABRAHAM LINCOLN Coloring Book

26_FORT STEVENS

Climb on a Civil War fort

Washington, DC was one of the most protected cities in the world during the Civil War. Sixty-eight forts with over nine-hundred cannons helped keep the city safe. Most of the forts have largely disappeared, except for Fort Stevens. Here, you can run up and down earthworks and touch giant cannons.

Fort Stevens played an important role in American history. On July 11, 1864, the Confederate Army stood outside of Washington, DC and Fort Stevens was the only thing that stood in between the army and The White House. As the Union soldiers defended DC, President Abraham Lincoln visited Fort Stevens. While there, he allegedly came under fire. If true, it's the only time a US President was attacked during battle. *Spoiler alert:* He was okay. When you visit, find the stone marker that denotes where President Lincoln stood when he visited Fort Stevens.

Every year, Fort Stevens hosts two celebrations. The first is in July to celebrate the anniversary of the Battle of Fort Stevens. There are Civil War reenactments, music, and dancing. A President Lincoln reenactor shows up and there's a demonstration on what medicine was like during the Civil War. A children's tent is set up with activities for all ages.

The second event is every September called Lincoln-Thomas Day. The celebration with music and kids' activities honors Elizabeth Thomas, a free Black woman who lost her farm and house to build Fort Stevens. The government later paid her for the land and returned it. Her legacy and contribution to US history is honored every year.

Address 6001 13th Street NW, Washington, DC 20011, www.nps.gov/places/fort-stevens.htm // **Getting there** Bus D40 to Georgia Avenue & Quackenbos Street NW // **Hours** Unrestricted // **Ages** 3+

TIP: Listen to live music during the summer months at Fort Dupont.

27_FREDERICK DOUGLASS HOUSE

Born into slavery, fought for freedom and justice

History books tell the tale of Frederick Douglass, one of DC's most important residents. Born into slavery, he escaped and became an influential abolitionist, fighting for freedom of all enslaved people. In 1877, Douglass and his wife Anna bought a mansion on a hill overlooking the city. Today, you can visit and see what their life was like in the 19th century.

While Frederick Douglass lived on Cedar Hill, he had 21 grandchildren, who were frequent visitors to the mansion. Despite his fame, Douglass was a grandfather first. Inside his home, he often gave piggyback rides and let his granddaughters braid his hair.

Go on a free tour of the Frederick Douglass House and see how a large family lived. At the front of the house are two parlors. The east parlor was for entertaining guests, but the west one was for family. Douglass would play the violin and piano, sing, and dance with his grandchildren. His original piano is still in the parlor. Also in the west parlor are binoculars for you to use to spot native birds and views of the US Capitol and Washington Monument.

TIP: The Mary McLeod Bethune Council House is the home of another activist.

Head to the dining room and find the old ice cream machine. A lover of the frozen treat, Douglass often made vanilla ice cream for his grandchildren. Go to the upstairs bedrooms and notice the chamber pots. With no restrooms inside, these pots were used for the Douglasses to go to the bathroom in the middle of the night. The next morning it was often the youngest grandchild's job to empty the pots. Imagine that!

Address 1411 W Street Southeast, Washington, DC 20020, +1 (771) 208-1499, www.nps.gov/frdo/index.htm // **Getting there** Metro to Anacostia (Green Line) // **Hours** See website for seasonal hours // **Ages** 3+

28_GAME OF FROGS

Hop around to find hidden amphibian statues

If you spot a small frog statue while exploring DC, you're not seeing things. There are almost 200 frog statues painted in all the colors of the rainbow hidden throughout the city. They are down alleys, in trees, sitting on lamp posts. They really are everywhere! You know when you spot one because each one has "Game of Frogs" etched into the statue. Some are attached, while others can be picked up.

Why are frog statues hidden throughout the nation's capital? It's because of a man named Andrew and his boredom. During the height of the COVID-19 pandemic, Andrew wanted to inspire people to go outside safely. He created a mold and made a handful of frog statues from concrete. He painted them different colors – red, yellow, purple. Then he hid them in safe and accessible places. Many are in spots where kids find them before adults.

Andrew calls his "Game of Frogs" a "city-wide game of nonsense." It's a way for visitors and locals to have fun while out for a walk. If you find one, snap a photo and share it with the Instagram account called "GameofFrogs." Andrew will share it with his followers for others to find too.

Some notable places with "Game of Frog" statues are the Tidal Basin, especially during the popular Cherry Blossom Festival. Pocket parks and popular streets lined with restaurants are usual places to find one or two. If you have trouble finding one, don't worry. Andrew makes a new batch every once in a while and hides them around the city, and now in nearby Baltimore too.

Address Various locations, www.instagram.com/gameoffrogs // **Getting there** Varies by location // **Hours** Unrestricted // **Ages** 3+

TIP: Also look for the "Empathy" signs on electric poles throughout the city.

29_GEORGETOWN CANAL BOATS

Take a boat ride back in time

Mules pulled boats through the Chesapeake & Ohio (C&O) Canal to transport people and goods into Georgetown in the 19th century. Usually, the canal boat operators lived on their boats with their families, and their children would often walk barefoot through the mud to guide the mules as they pulled the boats along. What a messy job! You'll see photos of the scene on the Georgetown Canal Boat Tour.

The Georgetown Canal Boat Tour is a unique experience even though the boats are no longer pulled by mules! It's an hour-long ride along the historic C&O Canal. Moving slowly through the water, it's a gentle ride, but the start of the tour is thrilling. The canal boat goes through what's called a lock. Guides use a key to open a gate in a 19th-century stone wall for the boat to go through. The gate is heavy, so it takes two or three people to push it open! Once the boat is inside, the lock fills up with rushing water, rocking the boat back and forth. The air is cool and smells like a damp basement. Once the water raises the boat around 15 feet, another gate opens, and the boat continues on toward the Key Bridge. It feels like an elevator ride.

A guide points out famous sites in Georgetown and talks about life on a canal boat. Lock keys and mule harnesses are pulled out for you to touch. The guide even talks about what food families ate while living on the small canal boats – eels and turtles are just a few meals on the menu. The seats spin around, so you can see everything around you.

Address 1057 Thomas Jefferson Street NW, Washington, DC 20007, +1 (202) 480-9540, www.georgetownheritage.org/tour-experiences // **Getting there** Metro to Foggy Bottom-GWU (Blue, Orange, Silver Lines) // **Hours** Apr–Oct Wed–Sun 10am, noon, 2pm & 4pm // **Ages** 3+

TIP: Play games from colonial times at the nearby Old Stone House.

30_GIANT ADIRONDACK CHAIR

Where an enormous person might relax

There are two giant chairs in DC, and you're allowed to climb on one of them. On the spacious lawn of the Duke Ellington School of the Arts is a giant, green Adirondack chair. Even when school is out, kids still like to hang out on the chair. The good news is that it's open to anyone, so you are welcome to climb up and relax or snap a photo with a friend.

But how did this giant chair appear in the lawn of a Washington, DC school? Artist Joel Edward Sisson created six giant Adirondack chairs with disadvantaged youth in the Twin Cities: Minneapolis and Saint Paul. They were placed around the two cities before making their way to other parts of the country. One was brought to DC for an art installation and then donated to the Duke Ellington School. It's been restored, and Washingtonians have enjoyed its presence for years.

It's appropriate that the giant Adirondack chair rests on the Duke Ellington campus. The school is named after famous jazz musician and composer Duke Ellington, a native Washingtonian. Ellington was an artist who had big thinking. It's what led him to becoming a jazz icon. In a similar way, the chair reminds kids to always think big. What big ideas can you come up with as you climb up and get comfortable on the chair? Maybe you'll change modern music as we know it like Duke Ellington did, or dream up an innovation like many people from DC have in the past. Or think big by inviting your friends to see how many people can fit on the giant Adirondack chair.

Address 3500 R Street NW, Washington, DC 20007, +1 (202) 282-0123 // **Getting there** Bus D6 to Reservoir Road & 35th Street NW // **Hours** Unrestricted // **Ages** 3+

TIP: Explore the Children's Section at the nearby Georgetown Neighborhood Library.

31_GIANT GUMBALL MACHINE

Free gum inside a grand hotel

This fancy hotel isn't just for adults. Hidden among the chandelier and marble columns at the Riggs Hotel are surprises to discover. Down a winding staircase near the lobby is a giant gumball machine filled with gumballs in all colors. In fact, the gumball machine can hold between 70,000 and 75,000 gumballs, and they're free! There's a bowl near the machine with tokens for all to use. Pop the token in the machine, turn, and watch your gumball spiral into your hand. Grab two gumballs to blow the perfect bubble.

The gumball machine is whimsical inside a hotel with a deep history. The downtown building first opened in 1891 as Riggs Bank and was called the "Bank of Presidents." Twenty-three US presidents banked here, including Abraham Lincoln. American Red Cross founder Clara Barton and suffragist Susan B. Anthony also had bank accounts. Money stored in Riggs Bank helped finance Robert Peary's first expedition to the North Pole in 1909, the US Capitol's expansion, and the purchase of Alaska from Russia.

Riggs Bank is now Riggs Hotel, but it's not hard to uncover its past. Near the gumball machine is the bank's original vault, which you can touch – the hotel was designed for anything to be touched. You can even pet the porcelain cat sculptures near the old vault!

On the main floor, you'll feel small looking up at the 22-foot-tall ceilings. Inside the hotel's café is a two-story glass case with larger-than-life flowers inside. Snap a photo by it to see how the flowers tower over you.

Address 900 F Street NW, Washington, DC 20004, +1 (202) 638-1800, www.riggsdc.com // Getting there Metro to Gallery Place-Chinatown (Green, Red, Yellow Lines) // Hours Unrestricted // Ages 5+

TIP: Enjoy a unique sensory experience at the nearby Museum of Illusions.

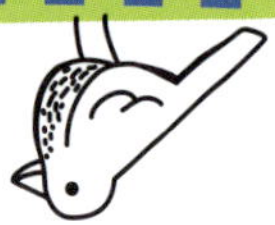

32_GLASS FOREST

Enchantment among the trees

Enchanting forests aren't just in fairytales – there's an actual one in DC! The Glass Forest is a special place filled with whimsical sculptures and art installations. There's a praying mantis made from bamboo hanging on a tree. Pieces of mirrors and CDs (ask your parents what those are) dangle from branches. At every turn, there's something that makes you stop, look, and squeal with delight.

The Glass Forest is hidden. Next to the Palisades Recreation Center is a tiny dirt path. Follow it for a few feet until you see another trail leading into the forest. Then step inside, and you'll find many works of art, most made from natural and recycled materials. Look for the wind chimes made with wood and metal. Search for the all-blue statue of a man in a suit and tie.

As you explore the Glass Forest, it's easy to wonder how such a place came to be. Enter James McMahon. When Jimmy Carter was president at the end of the 1970s, McMahon decided to transform an unused piece of land into an art space for the community. An artist himself, he created most of the sculptures inside the Glass Forest. Other artists have added to the space over time.

McMahon has a two-fold mission for the Glass Forest. First, he wants kids everywhere to put down technology, get out of the house, and explore the world around them. Secondly, he wants you to know that anyone can be an artist. Many of his sculptures are made from materials found in the forest. Can you imagine what you might make with a few pieces of wood?

Address 5200 Sherier Place NW, Washington, DC 20016 // **Getting there** D84 to MacArthur Boulevard NW & Edmunds Place NW // **Hours** Unrestricted // **Ages** 5+

TIP: The nearby Palisades Playground honors the Indigenous people who first lived along the Potomac River.

33_GO-GO MUSEUM & CAFÉ

Dance to DC's official music

DC actually has an official type of music, and it's called go-go. To learn all about it, visit Anacostia's Go-Go Museum & Café. Step inside the two-floor museum, and you may meet Ronald Moten. People call him "Moe," and he's dedicated his life to preserving, celebrating, and teaching all about go-go music.

Musician Chuck Brown created the essential sounds of go-go in the mid-1960s, a special type of funk music using live instrumentation, call and response, and different percussion instruments like congas and cowbells. Residents on the streets surrounding the Go-Go Museum & Café would blast the music loudly, and you can often hear it at block parties and celebrations around town even today. Modern streetwear was born out of the go-go movement.

To begin your museum experience, find the digital screens that depict go-go icons, like "Big G" and "Sugar Bear," and ask them questions about the music. For example, you can find out which Hollywood movies feature go-go, like *School Daze* (1988) and *Streetwise* (1984). You'll hear tunes throughout the museum, including an entire station celebrating women in go-go, like Be'la Dona.

Once you're ready to go big time, find the stage on the lower levels and belt out your own go-go song. You can also create digital public art using a virtual spray can. After all, public art goes hand in hand with go-go music. Don't miss the outdoor courtyard, the café that sells street food from the African Diaspora, and the restrooms wallpapered with go-go posters.

Address 1920 Martin Luther King Jr. Avenue SE, Washington, DC 20020, +1 (202) 848-4394, www.gogomuseumcafe.com, info@gogomuseumcafe.com // Getting there Metro to Anacostia (Green & Yellow Lines) // Hours Guided tours by online reservation only; self-guided tours: Wed & Sat 10am–6pm // Ages 4+

TIP: Play on the pirate ship-themed playground in nearby Anacostia Park.

34_HABESHA MARKET & CARRY OUT

Where you can eat with your hands

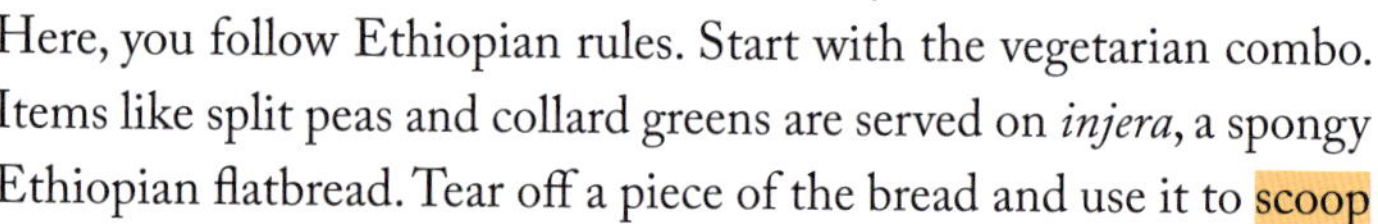

You may get in trouble for eating with your hands at home, but not at Habesha Market & Carry Out. Here, you follow Ethiopian rules. Start with the vegetarian combo. Items like split peas and collard greens are served on *injera*, a spongy Ethiopian flatbread. Tear off a piece of the bread and use it to scoop up the food – no forks or spoons needed. For the most authentic experience, eat with your right hand only like kids in Ethiopia.

Family-owned since 2005, Habesha Market is a great way to experience food from another country. It's open every day for breakfast, lunch, and dinner. In addition to the regular menu, there's a buffet with dishes you can see and smell before tasting, like *sambusas*, crispy pastries filled with lentils or beef.

Breakfast is served all day. Scrambled eggs and egg sandwiches are on the menu, but you should try the more traditional dishes. There's *ful*, fava beans flavored with tomatoes, garlic, lemon juice, parsley, and olive oil. *Kinche* is a porridge similar to oatmeal. When in doubt, ask one of the servers for suggestions. They're more than happy to explain all about Ethiopian food.

The area surrounding Habesha is sometimes called "Little Ethiopia" because many people from Ethiopia have moved here, starting in the 1970s. Today, the largest Ethiopian community outside of Africa lives in DC and its suburbs. So Ethiopian restaurants are plentiful here. You can take some more dishes home with you and buy fresh *injera* any time at the small market inside Habesha.

Address 1919 9th Street Northwest, Washington, DC 20001, +1 (202) 232-1919, www.habeshamarket.com, contact@habeshamarket.com // **Getting there** Metro to Shaw-Howard University (Green & Yellow Lines) // **Hours** Daily 8am–10pm // **Ages** 3+

TIP: Visit the African American Civil War Memorial nearby.

35_HILLWOOD ESTATE

This mansion has a pink bathroom

It's not every day you get to explore a mansion. Hillwood Estate, Museum & Gardens was one of the homes of Marjorie Merriweather Post, a cereal company heiress and often considered the richest woman in the US during her lifetime. Today, her grand house is open for all to visit.

There's a lot to find inside the mansion. You can open the cabinets in the kitchen where lavish meals were prepared for Post's dinner guests. Look at fashion-forward dresses in her personal closet. And explore her pink bathroom with pink tiles, pink bath mat, and even a pink toilet! Amidst the mansion's gold and gems, the house sparkles.

Even though you have to be gentle inside, you can run free in the mansion's gardens. Spread across 13 acres, the Japanese-style garden features waterfalls, stepping stones, and wooden bridges. If you're lucky, you may see Cecilia the red-eared slider turtle, or Oscar the northern water snake. (Don't worry – neither bites.) The gardens have green spaces for picnics, a greenhouse with orchids in bloom every March, fountains, a pet cemetery, and a brightly colored *dacha*, or Russian summer house.

Pick up one of four treasure hunts at Guest Services. Each hunt leads you to places like Post's safe inside her closet, where she kept her fancy jewelry, and the many animal statues in the gardens. There's a small prize if you complete the hunt. To continue the fun, come back for Crêpe Days, a French holiday celebrating the midpoint between winter and spring with yummy crêpes.

Address 4155 Linnean Avenue NW, Washington, DC 20008, +1 (202) 686-5807, www.hillwoodmuseum.org // **Getting there** Metro to Van Ness-UDC (Red Line) // **Hours** Tue–Sun 10am–5pm // **Ages** 2+

TIP: Go on a light hike at nearby Western Ridge Trail along Rock Creek.

36_HIRSHHORN ART SCHOOL

Think like an artist

One of the most whimsical museums along the National Mall is inside a doughnut-shaped building. If that's not enough to entice you to walk inside the Hirshhorn Museum and Sculpture Garden, the giant, polka-dotted pumpkin sculpture by Japanese artist Yayoi Kusama will.

Once inside, you'll find the Hirshhorn Art School, a large space where kids of all ages can create art for free. On Wednesdays, they host one of the city's most interactive story times. It starts with free play in the gallery, where kids can play among famous works of art. Enjoy story time with a staff member, and then you can create your own art in the studio. For example, in honor of polka-dot-loving artist Yayoi Kusama's 96th birthday, the story time book was about circles. Then the kids created their own masterpieces using circles.

Saturday is open studio day at the art school. For four hours, anyone can pop in and create all sorts of art. Activities are usually themed around the museum exhibits. Sometimes it's painting, and other times it's making posters. Supplies are provided, and staff members are eager to help if needed. The space has comfy couches just for hanging out. It's also a museum in and of itself. Artifacts are on display related to the museum's exhibits. During the exhibit of graffiti-inspired artist Jean-Michel Basquiat's work, his lab coat was on display at the art school. After you've created your own art, order soft-serve ice cream at Dolcezza, a local café inside the Hirshhorn.

Address Independence Avenue & 7th Street SW, Washington, DC 20560, +1 (202) 633-1000, hirshhorn.si.edu/explore/hirshhorn-art-school // **Getting there** Metro to L'Enfant Plaza (Blue, Green, Orange, Silver, Yellow Lines) // **Hours** Wed 10am–noon, Sat 10am–2pm // **Ages** 3+

TIP: Moongate Garden in the nearby Enid A. Haupt Garden is modeled after a Chinese temple.

37_ICE CREAM JUBILEE

Travel the world through ice cream

What's better than cookies-and-cream and chocolate-chip-cookie-dough ice cream? Both flavors in one scoop! Ice Cream Jubilee sells just that – cookies-and-cookie-dough ice cream. It's a crowd favorite, alongside flavors like marionberry with blackberries, butter cake, and lemon.

The smell of waffle cones baking brings in customers of all backgrounds, but the real magic is in this mom-owned ice cream shop's more unique flavors. Inspired by owner Victoria Lai's Asian heritage, flavors like matcha-green-tea and passionfruit-guava introduce kids to new tastes from around the world. You can travel the world just by eating ice cream!

It was Lai's dad who first inspired her love for ice cream. Growing up, her family ate it any time Lai's dad came home late from work. To make things even more fun, he challenged them to mix in their own ingredients and create different flavors.

When Lai came to DC to work at The White House, she started making ice cream as a creative outlet. After winning the popular vote at a local ice cream challenge, she turned her hobby into a full-time business.

Now she creates the cold deliciousness to bring a smile to her customers' faces, especially the littlest ones. A mother herself, Lai offers a special menu of Asia-inspired flavors during Asian American and Pacific Islander Heritage Month (May), hosts a summer reading club where kids get free ice cream for reading books, and gives a portion of profits back to the community.

Address 301 Water Street SE, #105, Washington, DC 20003, +1 (202) 863-0727, www.icecreamjubilee.com, info@icecreamjubilee.com // Getting there Metro to Navy Yard-Ballpark (Green & Yellow Lines) // Hours Sun–Thu noon–9pm, Fri & Sat noon–10pm // Ages 2+

TIP: Yards Park next door is a waterfront park with a boardwalk, splash area, and a summer concert series.

38_IMAGINATIONS

Step inside a tipi

What better way to learn than through play? That's the goal of the imagiNATIONS Activity Center inside the National Museum of the American Indian. For thousands of years, Native people called this land home, and they remain an important part of our nation. This museum is where you can learn about them and their cultures.

Every part of the imagiNATIONS Activity Center is interactive. Learn about Native housing by putting together a 3D *iglu* (spelled "iglu," not "igloo") puzzle or by stepping inside a tipi. You'll learn that, unlike what's shown in movies and books, tipis are made with many poles, not just three. The one inside the Activity Center is made from 13 poles. Tipis are more like community centers than homes. And they are also portable – some can be taken down and moved within five minutes!

Many everyday items were invented by Native peoples. For example, the Inuit people in Alaska and Canada made glasses from bone to protect their eyes in the snow – these snow glasses inspired sunglasses. Common foods that originally came from North America and were stewarded by Native peoples include pumpkins, corn, and sunflowers.

Most of the activities here are low technology to encourage you to disconnect from devices. Each activity is meant to be experienced, touched, and felt. The one exception is the skateboarding station, where you ride a virtual skateboard through a digital skate park. Skateboarding was inspired by Hawaiian surfing and is a popular sport within many Native cultures today.

Address 4th Street & Independence Avenue SW, Washington, DC 20560, +1 (202) 633-1000, americanindian.si.edu/visit/dc/activity-center // Getting there Metro to Federal Center SW (Blue, Orange, Silver Lines) // Hours Museum: Daily 10am–5:30pm; Activity Center: Tue–Sat 10am–4pm // Ages 2+

TIP: See what's blooming in the Children's Garden at the US Botanic Garden.

39_IMMIGRANT FOOD

Try food from around the world at Union Market

Where do your ancestors come from? It's a question everyone asks when they walk into Immigrant Food, a popular restaurant celebrating the country's immigrant history, legacy, and community. It's a question meant to be discussed among families over good food. After all, people have gathered around meals for centuries as families, friends, and communities.

There are two menus at Immigrant Food, but only one has food selected from every corner of the globe. You can have fries from Belgium, a sandwich with three kinds of meat from Cuba, chicken wings from Greece, and even churros with dipping chocolate from Ecuador.

The other menu is called an "Engagement Menu," with different ways people can help immigrants. This menu changes, but some past ways to engage include reading a book or listening to a podcast about immigrant stories, or giving money to local organizations doing good.

Owned by immigrants and employing mostly immigrants from around the world, Immigrant Food honors the immigrant legacy of the United States of America. Except for Indigenous Peoples, all Americans originally come from somewhere else. Immigrant Foods helps families create memories around food while also learning about different cultures. To make it fun, each plate pops with color, and there are different facts about immigrants on the back of the coasters. Of the four locations, this one is unique because it's inside Union Market, the city's largest food hall with international foods, shops, and regular events.

Address 1309 5th Street NE, Washington, DC 20002, +1 (202) 888-0760, www.immigrantfood.com // **Getting there** Metro to NoMa-Gallaudet U (Red Line); bus 92 to Florida Avenue & 5th Street NE // **Hours** Sun–Thu 11am–8pm, Fri & Sat 11am–9pm // **Ages** 2+

TIP: Try Central and Latin American cuisine at La Cosecha.

40_INTERNATIONAL SPY MUSEUM

Go under cover on a secret mission

Never reveal your real name at the International Spy Museum, the world's largest collection of espionage artifacts. Before you begin your visit, you're given a fake name, a fake hometown, and a mission, all on a special spy badge that you can keep. Throughout the museum are stations where you'll tap your badge to uncover parts of your unique mission. A border guard quizzes you on your cover identity. Another station uses artificial intelligence to create disguises. Pick your gender, age, and accessories as part of the disguise, or use the station to see what you may look like in a few decades.

Once you complete your mission, a computer gives you your top spy skills. As you weave through the Spy Museum, you'll find elements that will test those skills. Crawl through a real air duct quietly to test your stealthiness. Do you have a good grip? See how long you can hang onto a bar above the ground.

Be sneaky and learn all the devices spies used to conceal things, like cameras as buttons or a transmitter inside tiger poop. Learn about unexpected spies, like pigeons. During World War I, soldiers tied cameras onto pigeons to spy on the enemy from above. One spy pigeon even won a top military award for saving countless lives.

TIP: See Cher Ami, the spy pigeon, at the National Museum of American History.

Don't leave before stopping into the museum store. Among the usual gifts and apparel there are spy gadgets, including a pen with invisible ink, sunglasses that show what's behind you, and a megaphone that picks up whispers in another room. Is espionage in your future?

Address 700 L'Enfant Plaza Southwest, Washington, DC 20024, +1 (202) 393-7798, www.spymuseum.org, info@spymuseum.org // **Getting there** Metro to L'Enfant Plaza (Blue, Green, Orange, Silver, Yellow Lines) // **Hours** See website for seasonal hours // **Ages** 4+

SPY
ONE WAY

41_THE JOKES PHONE

Laugh with friends

Can you imagine a world without cell phones? Your parents probably can! Before everyone was connected through cell phones, they'd use the pay phones that were on many street corners. If you needed to call someone, you put a few coins in the slot, and you dialed your friend's phone number. Pay phones are a thing of the past, but in Chevy Chase, along a street lined with houses, you'll find the Jokes Phone. You can't call anyone from it, but you can hear a bunch of funny jokes!

Built by a substitute teacher at a local elementary school, this 1991 pay phone from Taiwan is rewired to keep you laughing. Attached to the phone is an old-school phonebook with instructions. Pick up the handle and dial "1" to hear a knock-knock joke. Press "2" for little-kid jokes, "3" for jokes for slightly older kids, and "4" for clean jokes for older kids and adults. After you're done cracking up, maybe you can come up with a joke of your own. Then dial "0" to leave a voicemail for the phone's creator. He may even add your joke to the phone's joke collection!

TIP: Broad Branch Market nearby is a popular place to get ice cream.

"What did the mother corn say to her children? Don't forget to wash behind your ears." That's one joke from the phone, but it has more than just jokes up its sleeves. Dial "5" or "6" to learn fun facts, like "Did you know that most people can't lick their elbows?" Press "7," "8," or "9" to hear positive thoughts that will brighten your day. "This moment is temporary," or "School's fun" are just two positive thoughts from this irresistible pay phone.

Address 3413 Northampton Street NW, Washington, DC 20015 // **Getting there** Bus C83 to McKinley Street & Chevy Chase Parkway NW // **Hours** Daily 6am–10pm // **Ages** 4+

Jokes
5-10-25
U.S. COINS ONLY
COIN RELEASE
Local Calls
0¢
operated by:
Pa Bell
PUSH FOR COIN

42_KENILWORTH AQUATIC GARDENS

Spot the colorful flowers – and birds too

Look in any tree at Kenilworth Aquatic Gardens, and see if you spot anything that's red or blue. It's probably a cardinal or a blue jay, just two of over 250 birds and more than 40 species that travel through Kenilworth Aquatic Gardens throughout the year. If you stand still, you may even hear their songs. Two decades after the Civil War, Union soldier Walter B. Shaw planted waterlilies from his native Maine on the land. His daughter Helen Shaw Fowler later expanded the gardens before ownership transferred to the National Park Services. Today, the gardens are an oasis in the middle of the city for all nature lovers.

If you're new to birdwatching, the birds make it easy. Borrow a pair of high-quality binoculars from the visitor center when they're open and walk the gardens' trails. Look for sparrows, hawks, geese, ducks, and many other feathered friends. If you want help identifying the birds, show up at 8:30am any Tuesday for a guided walk with a bird expert. Birdwatching walks are also offered every first Saturday and Sunday of the month.

Tall birds like green herons and great egrets stop here during migration. March through June marks spring migration, and the fall migration happens between August and November. Some birds make the gardens their home year-round, like red-winged blackbirds and Canada geese. If you go during the spring migration, you'll see lotus and waterlilies in bloom. The pink water flowers are beautiful!

Address 1550 Anacostia Avenue NE, Washington, DC 20019, +1 (202) 692-6080, www.nps.gov/keaq // **Getting there** Metro to Deanwood (Orange Line) // **Hours** Daily 8am–4pm // **Ages** 2+

TIP: Bike along nearby Anacostia Riverwalk Trail.

43_KILROY WAS HERE

Find hidden cartoons

Millions visit the World War II Memorial along the National Mall, but most people miss the hidden *Kilroy Was Here* cartoons. Created by plane inspectors during World War II, *Kilroy Was Here* memes became a symbol of resilience among American soldiers. Depicting a bald man with a long nose peeking over a wall with his fingers clutching the wall, *Kilroy Was Here* was graffitied throughout Europe and the Pacific during the war. A subtle way to honor the 16 million Americans who served during World War II, two *Kilroy Was Here* cartoons are at the famous memorial. One is near the Pennsylvania pillar and the other near the Delaware pillar.

Once you find the two *Kilroys,* spend time looking all around the World War II Memorial. Surrounding a fountain where some visitors cool their feet during hot months are 56 granite pillars representing every US state and territory. See if you can find your own home state's pillar.

Facing the Lincoln Memorial is the Freedom Wall. Gold stars, 4,048 of them here, each represent 100 Americans who sacrificed their lives during World War II. "Here we mark the price of freedom" is etched on the wall.

If you're lucky, you'll run into an actual World War II veteran. National Park Service rangers greet each veteran by saying, "Welcome to your memorial." And it's true – the memorial was created for them. The inclusion of *Kilroy Was Here* on the memorial is a nod to all American soldiers who fought for their country. It is both a funny cartoon and a symbol of their service.

Address 1750 Independence Avenue SW, Washington, DC 20024, +1 (202) 426-6841, www.nps.gov/wwii/index.htm // **Getting there** Metro to Smithsonian (Blue, Orange, Silver Lines) // **Hours** Unrestricted // **Ages** 2+

TIP: See ducks swimming in the Lincoln Memorial Reflecting Pool.
KILROY WAS HERE

44_KINGMAN & HERITAGE ISLANDS

Escape the city without leaving it

To see cranes, herons, and 100 other species of birds, head to Kingman & Heritage Islands, human-made islands in the Anacostia River. Located just off a popular trail, a boardwalk takes you over the water from Heritage Island to the larger Kingman Island, offering views of the Metro trains passing nearby. It feels like you've stumbled upon a secret island, and the treasures you'll find here are the animals.

Along the boardwalk bridges are signs with pictures of the wildlife to look out for: Canada geese, ducks, and even the occasional bald eagle, the biggest prize of them all! Look closely in the water to find frogs, turtles, and even wood ducks with their green and blue heads. Bring binoculars or simply look with your eyes, using the signs along the trail as a guide. Bald eagles are rare sightings, but blue herons aren't. Often standing tall in the water, they can be found any time of the year and look like dinosaurs popping out of the river.

The path continues through Kingman Island, where you'll find picnic tables along the Anacostia River. Pack a picnic and wave to passing boats. For more fun, there's a Little Free Library with nature-focused books near the entrance.

Over the years, many ideas were proposed on how to change the two islands. One of the wildest ones was to build a children's amusement park. Luckily, rather than roller coasters and Ferris wheels, the islands remain a natural oasis for both humans and wildlife to explore and enjoy!

Address 575 Oklahoma Avenue NE, Washington, DC 20002, +1 (202) 488-0627, www.kingmanisland.com, kingmanisland@livingclassroomsdc.org // **Getting there** Metro to Stadium Armory (Blue, Orange, Silver Lines) // **Hours** Daily dawn–dusk // **Ages** 0+

TIP: Meet the people who grow your food at the nearby RFK Stadium Open Air Farmers' Market.

45_KOGOD COURTYARD

Splash in a museum fountain

Not all museums are serious. You should be on your best behavior in the National Portrait Gallery's Hall of Presidents, where you will see paintings of every US president in history, but you can let loose in the Kogod Courtyard, a large space connecting the National Portrait Gallery and the Smithsonian American Art Museum. If you look closely at the courtyard's floor, you'll find two pools of water tempting you to jump in. And it's allowed! Take off your shoes and socks and splash around. It's serious fun!

After you've run around in the Kogod Courtyard's fountain, look up. You're in one of Washington, DC's most beautiful courtyards and one of the biggest indoor spaces in the city. The ceiling reaches high into the sky, with a glass ceiling that curves like the waves in the ocean. Light pours into the courtyard. Little gardens with plants and flowers fill the space. If you're hungry, there's a café that sells snacks, or you can eat a picnic at one of the tables.

Once you're dry from splashing, find the museum's kid-friendly corners. The "Explore!" room is a space just for you. Take turns tracing your silhouettes, strike a pose, and learn about emotions by building faces out of blocks. Through play, you'll learn about portraits and ask yourself questions like, "How do I see myself?" Across the hall is the Portrait Gallery Art Studio. Every weekend there are free, drop-in studio times to create all kinds of art, from painting to drawings. Whatever you create, you can take home!

Address 8th Street NW & G Street NW, Washington, DC 20001, +1 (202) 633-1000, npg.si.edu // Getting there Metro to Gallery Place-Chinatown (Green, Red, Yellow Lines) // Hours Daily 11:30am–7pm // Ages 1+

TIP: Catch a game or concert at Capital One Arena, a sensory-inclusive venue.

46_LABYRINTH GAMES & PUZZLES

The city's only store dedicated entirely to games

Before you can enter Labyrinth Games & Puzzles, there's a quiz. Written on a chalkboard sign at its entrance are two mind puzzles. Tell the person behind the register the right answer, and you'll win a little prize.

It's a fitting entrance to DC's only store entirely dedicated to games, and it's also owned by a mother. Back in 2012, Kathleen Donahue drove to the DC suburbs looking to purchase a Mancala board, a strategy game played with small stones. Returning to the city empty handed and stuck in traffic, she came up with the idea to start a game store in the city.

Profitable from the beginning, Labyrinth became a smash hit. LEGOs, jigsaw puzzles, card games, dominos – you'll find them all here. Today, it's a place where people of all ages want to hang out and browse through puzzles, games, and toys. There's always a puzzle out for anyone to help solve. A Q-BA-Maze is permanently set up by the side entrance, where kids drop marbles to see where they end up.

Knowledgeable staff members can recommend the best games for you. Tell them what you like, and you'll walk out with a new game that's guaranteed to be fun. Staff are good with gamers of all ages and remember the names of many visitors to the shop, which is one of the only board game stores in the country with a large selection dedicated to children.

TIP: Shop at the weekend Eastern Market flea market for food, toys, and more goodies.

There are regular events here for everybody, such as board-game nights and game clubs. And don't miss the used-game sale every September. Every event leaves guests happier than when they came in, which is the mission of the store.

Address 645 Pennsylvania Avenue SE, Washington, DC 20003, +1 (202) 544-1059, www.labyrinthdc.com // **Getting there** Metro to Eastern Market (Blue, Orange, Silver Lines) // **Hours** Mon noon–7pm, Tue, Thu & Fri 11am–10pm, Wed 11am–9pm, Sat & Sun 10am–7pm // **Ages** 2+

47_LANGDON SKATE PARK

Push your limits like Tony Hawk

Does the name Tony Hawk ring a bell? If you're into skateboarding, you know he's an icon and one of the greatest skateboarders of all time. There's even a video game series named after him. Turning his fame into a way to give back to the community, Hawk now helps build skate parks in urban settings around the country through the Tony Hawk Foundation, including one at the Langdon Recreation Center in Northeast DC. Bring your skateboard and try your hand at skateboarding tricks here at the Langdon Skate Park. After some practice, you may even get some air!

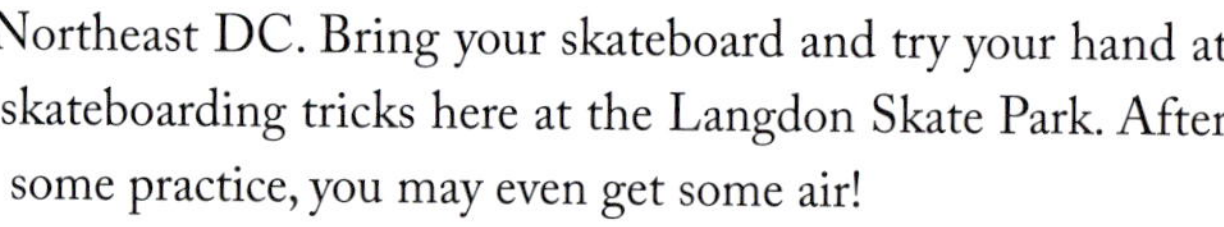

There are a handful of skate parks throughout Washington, DC. Some are bigger and more popular than the Langdon Skate Park, but the beauty here is its seclusion. It's easy to miss, which makes it a perfect place to practice your skateboarding skills unnoticed. The inside of the skate park is painted with graffiti art that changes on occasion.

Langdon Park is one of the city's biggest recreation spaces. There's a popular public pool nearby that's open from Memorial Day through Labor Day. The park also offers tennis courts, lots of grass to run around on, and the Chuck Brown Memorial, honoring an important figure in Washington, DC. Known as the "Godfather of Go-Go," Chuck Brown helped elevate go-go music, the city's official music that's a subgenre of the funk genre. If you walk around the statue, called *Wind Me Up Chuck* and created by Jackie Braitman, it looks like Chuck Brown's face is moving. It's a unique memorial!

Address 2901 20th Street NE, Washington, DC 20018, +1 (202) 576-6595, dpr.dc.gov/langdonpark // Getting there Bus C63 to Franklin & 22 Streets NE // Hours Unrestricted // Ages 5+

TIP: Another popular skate park is the Shaw Skate Park in Northwest DC.

48_LIBRARY ANIMAL MURALS

Read amidst a whimsical circus and orchestra

Have you ever seen an elephant licking ice cream, a monkey playing the cello, or a lion conducting an orchestra? Go to the children's section of the Mount Pleasant Neighborhood Library, one of the city's oldest libraries, and you can! Within two reading nooks are colorful murals painted by an artist named Aurelius Battaglia. If his art looks familiar, it's because Battaglia went on to help create some of Disney's most famous movies, including *Pinocchio*, *Dumbo*, and *Fantasia*.

Battaglia's story is an inspiring one. Born in DC, he was bedridden as a child due to an illness. To help him cope, his parents bought him coloring supplies. Eventually, he was able to make trips in a stroller. Often visiting the zoo, he started drawing animals, and the Mount Pleasant Neighborhood Library murals reflect his attention to detail. Look into the eyes of the brown bears wearing clothes. It's as if they stare back at you.

Before Battaglia worked at Disney, he used to trade his paintings for basic necessities, like getting his teeth cleaned. He drew cartoons for a few newspapers until he was asked to paint *Animal Circus* and *Animal Orchestra* inside the library as part of the Public Works of Art Program, a government initiative that helped give work to artists during the Great Depression. Just outside the library's children's section are signs that tell more about Battaglia's story.

Choose a Dr. Seuss book or a children's novel and sit down in one of the chairs in the nooks surrounded by the animals.

Address 3160 16th Street NW, Washington, DC 20010, +1 (202) 671-3121, www.dclibrary.org/plan-visit/mt-pleasant-library // Getting there Metro to Columbia Heights (Green & Yellow Lines) // Hours Sun 1–5pm, Mon–Wed 9am–8pm, Thu noon–8pm, Fri & Sat 10am–6pm // Ages 0+

TIP: Musician Frank O. Agbro hosts a children's concert from his nearby porch most Saturdays at 10:30am at 17th & Kilbourne Streets NW.

49_LIBRARY OF CONGRESS

Explore the world's largest library

Libraries are generally places that are full of books, and you have to be super quiet. Well, not the Library of Congress. Yes, there are over 38 million books here, but there's much more. The Library of Congress is also a museum with special nooks and corners for children to enjoy, like the "Collecting Memories: Treasures from the Library of Congress" exhibit.

Hosted inside one large room, the exhibit has something for everyone, but children often enjoy the part called "Guiding Memory," where you learn how students memorized their lessons throughout the centuries. For example, you'll find sheet music from a drummer boy during the Civil War. Often, the drummer boys were 13 and 14 years old, and it was up to them to memorize the music they would play for the troops. And they had to get it right – one drum beat meant Union soldiers had to turn left, and another meant turn right. In some ways, it was actually these drummer boys who led the soldiers during the Civil War.

Another piece in the exhibit is an ancient tablet made of clay. It dates back almost 12,000 years to the days of Mesopotamia, where modern-day Iraq sits. These tablets taught people how to be scribes, those who copied books by hand before printers were invented. Can you read what's on the tablets? Imagine what school would be like with tablets rather than books!

TIP: Next door is the Supreme Court, with giant pillars outside and a museum inside.

Don't miss the Main Reading Room, with its high ceiling and its walls covered with many books and sculptures. You can also attend live events of all kinds. They always have spaces for children, too!

Address 101 Independence Avenue SE, Washington, DC 20540, +1 (202) 707-5000, www.loc.gov // **Getting there** Metro to Capitol South (Blue, Orange, Silver Lines) // **Hours** Tue, Wed, Fri, & Sat 10am–5pm, Thu 10am–8pm // **Ages** 5+

50_LINCOLN'S COTTAGE

Take a tour of "Lincoln's Wild Home"

Can you imagine what life would be like if your mom or dad were the President of the United States of America? It's not easy to visit The White House, but you can get a taste of the life of a First Family at President Lincoln's Cottage, where President Abraham Lincoln, his wife Mary Todd Lincoln, and their sons spent many months, especially during the summer.

The cottage still stands on what was then a rural area and on high ground to help escape the city's summer heat. It's here where Lincoln and his family experienced a more normal life. Lincoln's youngest son Tad ran free, climbed trees, and played with family pets, including ponies and even peacocks! There was a working farm with cows and chickens too.

One of the best self-guided tours of President Lincoln's Cottage is the "Lincoln's Wild Home" Tour. Following a map and an audio guide, you have to find each stop on the tour like a scavenger hunt. Look for the life-sized statue of Lincoln and his horse Old Bob. You can see how tall you are compared to the president, who stood six feet and four inches tall. Lincoln and Tad often played checkers on the veranda. And Tad's pet goat "Nanny" was returned to The White House after the gardener complained about plants in the cottage garden being destroyed. On the daily guided tours, you can go inside the cottage to see where the family slept.

The cottage also hosts annual events, like a bluegrass music festival and a homecoming event with a petting zoo.

Address 140 Rock Creek Church Road NW, Washington, DC 20011, +1 (202) 829-0436, www.lincolncottage.org, info@lincolncottage.org // **Getting there** Metro to Georgia Avenue-Petworth (Green & Yellow Lines) // **Hours** Daily 9:30am–4:30pm // **Ages** 5+

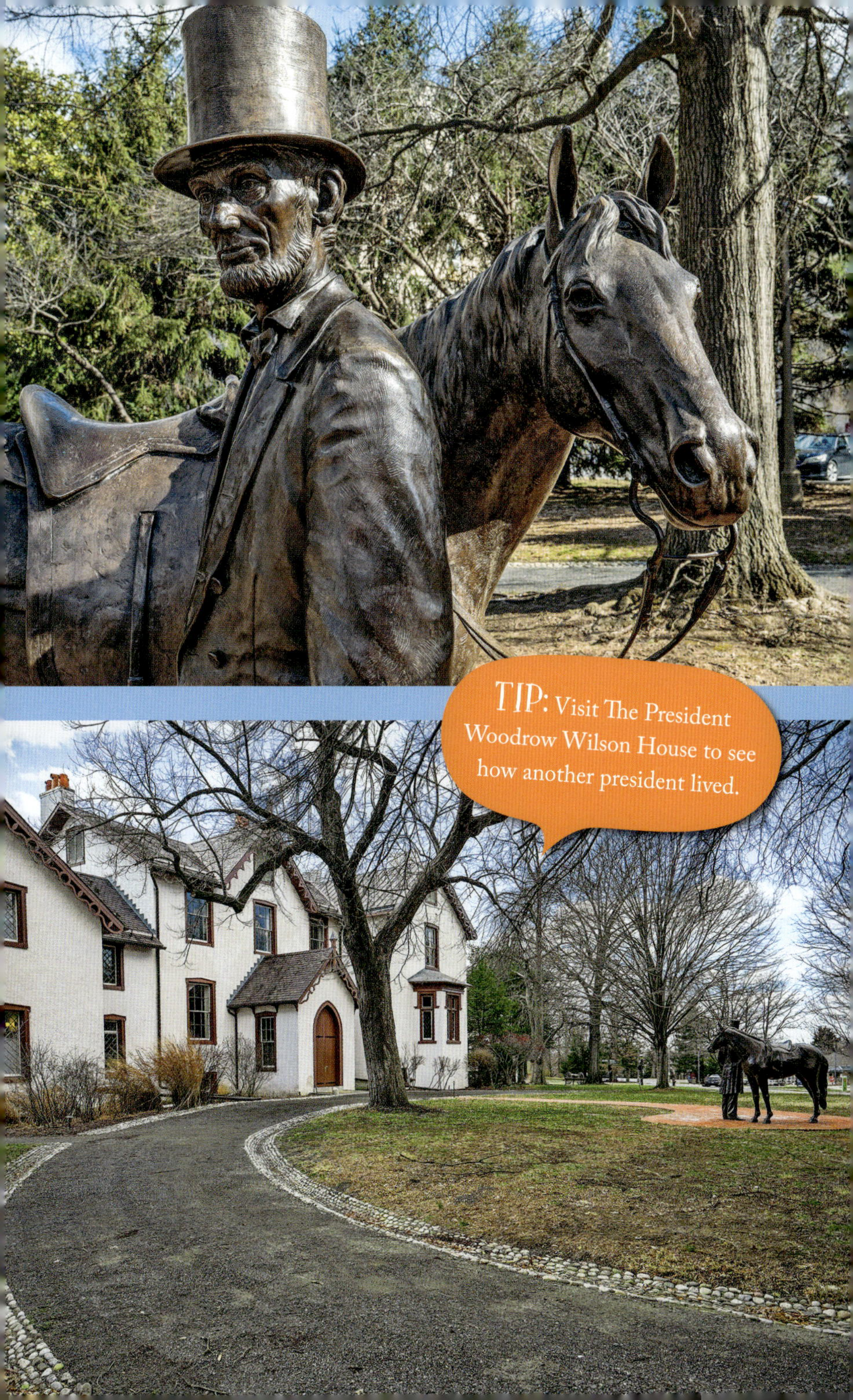
TIP: Visit The President Woodrow Wilson House to see how another president lived.

51_LINCOLN'S HITCHING POST

Where President Lincoln did everyday things

Washington, DC is where most US presidents and their families have lived. They have walked its streets, shopped in its stores, and even attended some of its churches. But there's one place that brings President Abraham Lincoln to life today, and that's the New York Avenue Presbyterian Church.

This 19th-century church is where the president and his family regularly attended services, and you can still find remnants of Lincoln's daily life here. Just outside is a seemingly mundane black pole. The small plaque points out that the pole is a hitching post where Lincoln's horse waited while the president was in the church.

There's more history inside. You can pop in and request a tour from the person at the front desk. You'll see an early, handwritten draft by Lincoln of his first plan to end slavery before he wrote the Emancipation Proclamation. There's also a pair of scissors and a paper cutter owned and used by the 16th president that he gave as a gift to the minister here at the time. In the sanctuary is the pew that Lincoln's family rented. If you're lucky, the bells will ring in the tower while you're there. They were a gift from Lincoln's son's wife and daughter, the only memorial to Lincoln from his family.

It makes sense that Lincoln attended this church. The congregation carries on his legacy through their long history of civil rights activism. They also run some of the city's longest-standing programs helping young people and those experiencing homelessness.

Address 1313 New York Avenue NW, Washington, DC 20005, +1 (202) 393-3700, www.nyapc.org, adminoffice@nyapc.org // **Getting there** Metro to McPherson Square (Blue, Orange, Silver Lines) // **Hours** Mon–Fri 9am–3:30pm // **Ages** 4+

TIP: Nearby Franklin Park used to be a spring that supplied water to The White House.

52_MAGIC TREE BOX

A miniature world for hobbits

Just off popular 14th Street, filled with real-life shops and restaurants, is a garden box along the sidewalk filled with miniature shops and houses for families of little gnomes and fairies. It's easy to miss the Magic Tree Box, so be on the lookout for a tree with vines growing up it. Once you spot the tree, look down. You'll find yellow- and green-painted steps leading to a gnome house. And a frog reads a book while sitting on a turtle in a pond. Moss grows as grass, and flowers and plants spring into the air.

How did this tiny world of wonders begin outside a historic rowhouse in a popular part of Washington, DC? It all started when a local man named Art noticed garden boxes in disrepair across the city. Many didn't have flowers inside of them or anything at all to look at. He started to wonder how he could turn his own garden box into a place where neighbors wanted to stop. So he went to the store and came home with a little fairy door. Soon, he added more fairy and hobbit things to the tree box, and it grew and grew.

Today, there's an entire miniature village inside his garden box. To give you a reason to come back, he transforms the village for certain holidays. A witch hat-themed hobbit house appears every October for Halloween, and little houses in the shape of ornaments appear in December. Once, a miniature circus showed up to the Magic Tree Box, complete with a tiny booth with tickets for you to admire. LEGO figures, one of Art's favorite toys, make regular appearances.

Address 1429 R Street NW, Washington, DC 20009, www.instagram.com Memorial/Cardozo (Green /the_magic_tree_box // **Getting there** Metro to U Street/African-American Civil War (Green & Yellow Lines) // **Hours** Unrestricted // **Ages** 2+

TIP: Walk two blocks south to see the Barbie Pond on Avenue Q.

53_MARVIN GAYE REC CENTER

Climb on musical instruments

Forget the regular, old jungle gym. You can climb on guitars, saxophones, and music notes at the Marvin Gaye Playground at the Marvin Gaye Recreation Center. It's an appropriate playground for a city that produced some of the country's greatest musicians. Jazz icon Duke Ellington was born near George Washington University. Parks and streets are named after Chuck Brown, the "Godfather of Go-Go Music," a subgenre of funk music from Washington, DC.

The Marvin Gaye Playground honors another great DC musician: Marvin Gaye. Hits like "How Sweet It Is (To Be Loved by You)" and "I Heard It Through the Grapevine" earned Gaye a place in music history. He helped define the voice of Motown, one of the biggest music labels today. Gaye's music is a little bit of soul, a little R&B, gospel, funk, and pop. Ask your parents who Stevie Wonder is because Marvin Gaye inspired his music.

TIP: Stroll along the trail that hugs the Watts Branch stream just beyond the rec center.

To help honor Marvin Gaye's legacy and impact on DC, a recreation center and playground were built blocks from one of his childhood homes. The playground is entirely enclosed and transforms into a splash park in hot months. A red guitar and yellow saxophone spray you with refreshing water. There are slides, sheets of music to climb on, and music notes you can ride on. Don't miss *What's Going On*, a grand statue of Marvin Gaye by Vinnie Bagwell, an artist who sculpts Black heroes, like abolitionist Frederick Douglass. Gaye's statue features an inscription that reads, "War is not the answer for only love can conquer hate."

Address 15 61st Street NE, Washington, DC 20019, +1 (202) 727-5432, dpr.dc.gov/marvingaye // Getting there Metro to Capitol Heights (Blue & Silver Lines) // Hours Unrestricted // Ages 0+

54_MATTHEW HENSON CENTER

Up close and personal with birds of prey

There are very few places where you can get close to birds of prey, or raptors, but the Matthew Henson Earth Conservation Center is one of them. Inside an old pump house along the Anacostia River, a raptor expert takes care of Sky, a red-tailed hawk, Devon, a barn owl, and Hurricane, a black vulture. When the center is open, you can meet and learn all about these amazing birds of prey.

Sky, Devon, and Hurricane, along with several other kinds of raptors, live at the Matthew Henson Center, named after one of the most famous Black explorers. Henson lived much of his life here in DC, but he loved going on adventures. As he grew up, he realized that he wanted to discover new places in the world. That desire took him to the Arctic many times. In fact, he claimed to be the first person to reach the North Pole.

To commemorate Matthew Henson, the Earth Conservation Corps, a non-profit dedicated to cleaning the Anacostia River, named this building after him. Look for the mosaic art piece in his honor that hangs on the outside of the center. And also see *Hanson the Heron*, a sculpture made from recyclable material pulled from the Anacostia River, and a reminder to keep our rivers clean and plastic-free.

The Earth Conservation Corps is all about repurposing things for good, including media and the arts. Another way they do this at the Henson Center is through building nests for osprey, large, fish-eating hawks that live along the Anacostia River. These nests are made out of old, upcycled guns.

TIP: Enjoy free fishing during Friday evenings in the summer at the nearby Monique Johnson Center.

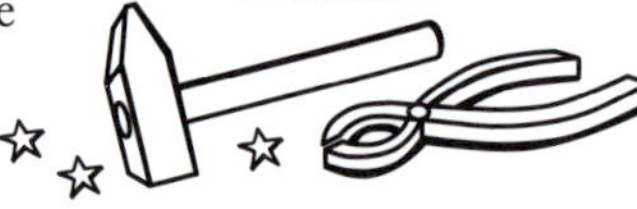

Address 2000 Half Street SW, Washington, DC 20024, +1 (202) 479-4505, www.earthconservationcorps.org // **Getting there** Bus C55 to 2nd & R Streets SW // **Hours** Mon–Fri 9am–5pm // **Ages** 2+

55_MERRY PIN

Make a mess while you craft

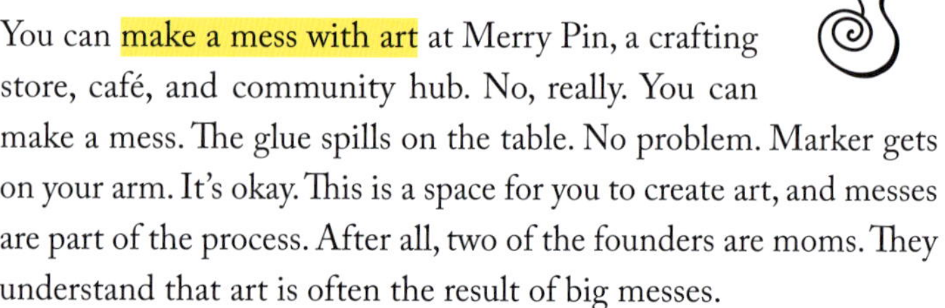

You can make a mess with art at Merry Pin, a crafting store, café, and community hub. No, really. You can make a mess. The glue spills on the table. No problem. Marker gets on your arm. It's okay. This is a space for you to create art, and messes are part of the process. After all, two of the founders are moms. They understand that art is often the result of big messes.

Walk inside this corner store along busy Georgia Avenue NW, and you're in a crafting wonderworld. Shelves are filled with all the supplies you need to create something beautiful: yarn, stickers, stationery, and so much more. Want to learn how to crochet? There's a starter kit for it. Need buttons for an art project? You can fill a bag for $1.50. Near the register are "Mystery Bags" filled with recycled craft supplies, like string, paper, gems, and other crafty goodies.

Climb the stairs to the second floor, where you'll find a crafting area with all the material you need to create your own art. From friendship bracelets to painted pottery, there's something for every artist. Need a break? Play with the dollhouse or draw on the chalkboard in the open room.

If you're hungry, order a yummy treat from the café. For savory cravings, get the ham and cheese croissant or an empanada, a hand pie filled with all sorts of things, like chicken and vegetables, enjoyed in different countries around the world. Or share a pickle plate with the whole family.

Have a sweet tooth? Try the rainbow marshmallow or a chocolate croissant.

Address 7350 Georgia Avenue NW, Washington, DC 20012, +1 (202) 204-1552, www.merrypindc.com, hello@merrypindc.com // Getting there Bus D40 to Georgia Avenue & Geranium Street NW // Hours Tue & Wed 10am–8pm, Thu–Sat 10am–9pm, Sun 10am–5pm // Ages 2+

TIP: Moh Moh Licious nearby serves momos, delicious dumplings from Nepal.

56_MILLENNIUM STAGE

Free concerts at the Kennedy Center

One of the fanciest things to do in DC is getting dressed up to go to the Kennedy Center, also known as the US National Cultural Center, that puts on plays, musical concerts, and more. People from all around the world visit the Kennedy Center to see the best musicians and artists perform. To make the arts more accessible, the Kennedy Center hosts free evening concerts on its Millennium Stage.

Billy Taylor, a well-known jazz pianist, was the first artist to perform on Millenium Stage in 1997. Thousands of others have played here since. Pop, classical, instrumental – music of all kinds hits the stage. One of the most impactful performances was the Afghan Youth Orchestra. Once the Taliban banned music in Afghanistan, the youth choir relocated to Portugal. They've played here twice.

Millennium Stage is designed for children. Performances last only one hour, giving kids the right amount of music to help them fall in love with the arts. Beyond music, Millennium Stage hosts events with authors of children's books, an outdoor movie series projecting classics like *Ratatouille*, festivals celebrating different holidays, and even a National Dance Day special.

Get to the Kennedy Center early so you can explore the grand building itself. Take the elevator to the rooftop to walk through an exhibit about President John F. Kennedy and learn why he loved the arts so much. Then walk outside to the spacious rooftop for city views and find the giant bust of President John F. Kennedy in the Grand Hall.

Address 2700 F Street NW, Washington, DC 20566, +1 (202) 416-8000, www.kennedy-center.org/whats-on/millennium-stage // **Getting there** Metro to Foggy Bottom-GWU (Blue, Orange, Silver Lines) // **Hours** Concerts: Wed–Sat 6–7pm // **Ages** 2+

TIP: Explore the gardens at the nearby Watergate Complex.

57_MILLER CABIN

Step inside a real log cabin

Log cabins are usually dwellings that you read about in storybooks or history class. But there's a real log cabin right here in Washington, DC, and it's a hidden one. If you hike along the Valley Trail in Rock Creek Park, the city's largest park and the nation's third designated national park, you'll walk past Miller Cabin. It's not a scene from a movie. This is a real cabin, and it tells a fun story.

Do you miss nature when you're in a big city like DC, where trees, open grass, and fields are harder to find? If the answer is yes, you're not alone. When poet Joaquin Miller came to DC in 1883, he preferred more rustic living. While others were building grand homes in the city, Miller built a log cabin, where he lived for two years. It was an odd sight to see a log cabin in the middle of a city! When it was threatened with demolition, a senator from California helped save it. The cabin was taken apart log by log and rebuilt in Rock Creek Park, where it stands today.

At first, the people used the Miller Cabin as a shelter from the rain. Then Miller's niece took over the cabin and turned it into a concession stand. For over 20 years, she sold candy and soda to park visitors. She even taught art classes in the cabin, according to the National Park Service website. Later, the Joaquin Miller Cabin Poetry Series used the cabin for its gatherings before they got popular and outgrew the space. Today, you can get up close to the log cabin and peek through its windows into the single room.

Address Picnic Area 6, 696 Beach Drive NW, Washington, DC 20011, www.nps.gov/places/joaquin-miller-cabin.htm // **Getting there** Bus D60 to 16th Street & Missouri Avenue NW // **Hours** Unrestricted // **Ages** 0+

TIP: Also in Rock Creek Park is Peirce Mill that ground grains in the 19th century.
TUPELO TREE
PLANTED BY
CAMP FIRE GIRLS
FIRST PRESIDENT

58_MIRACLE THEATRE

Watch family-friendly movies in an old theater

A movie theater with the word "miracle" in its title is bound to make magic happen. The Miracle Theatre shows second-run, favorite movies. Jasmine might show up before a showing of *Aladdin*. If *Frozen* is playing, Elsa may make an appearance for a photo-op. It's true magic!

Opened in 1909, the Miracle Theatre is the oldest movie theater in DC showing films and hosting live performances. In the 1960s, the theater was sold to a church, but it was restored as a theater in 2011. Today, it's a space for families to laugh and connect with each other with a rotating schedule of family-friendly movies.

You can see a movie here every Friday and Sunday afternoon. There's always a special summer movie series, and holiday movies play every December. The theater is even known to host a pajama party during a screening of *The Polar Express*. Walk inside, and you feel transported back in time. Adults will reminisce about the times they went to the movies with their own parents. A concession stand in the lobby sells goodies, including, of course, buttery popcorn. Strollers are welcome in this theater for the community.

Show your same-day ticket to four neighborhood restaurants, and they'll offer you nice discounts on your meals: Akeno Sushi Bar and Thai, Ambar, and Lavagna. Or show a receipt from one of the four restaurants to the theater, and you'll receive a discount on concessions to enjoy during your movie. And feel free to recommend your favorite movies for future screenings.

Address 535 8th Street SE, Washington, DC 20003, +1 (202) 400-3210, www.themiracletheatre.com, info@themiracletheatre.com // **Getting there** Metro to Eastern Market (Blue, Orange, Silver Lines) // **Hours** See website for movie and event schedule // **Ages** 5+

TIP: Follow the chicken-feet prints in the alley across the street to find bright murals.

59_MISSION MUFFINS

Yummy treats with a mission

Blueberry is the most popular flavor at Mission Muffins, but don't skip the chocolate, cinnamon, or apple muffins. There's even a chocolate-chip muffin affectionately named "A Milk Chocolate Chip Off The Old Block." Add banana to the muffin mix, and Mission Muffins calls it "Bananas And Milk (Chocolate Chips, That Is)."

Mission Muffins bakes yummy treats, and they are also on a mission to help people in need. Located inside a small trailer, Mission Muffins is a job-training program for Central Union Mission, one of the city's oldest non-profits helping people find homes, jobs, and clothes so they can be safe and happy. Because of the mission's inspiring work, thousands of DC residents now have better lives and brighter futures.

Here's how it works. Mission Muffins teaches people how to bake and sell muffins and interact with customers so that they can earn a stable income. These activities help them develop important skills in retail, customer service, and time management. Once the participants move on from Mission Muffins, they are ready to go out into the world as good employees elsewhere. Mission Muffins offers them a pathway to income and security.

TIP: Two blocks away is the iconic Union Station train terminal.

In addition to offering delicious muffins here, Mission Muffins serves "Mission Mud" coffee to adults, of course, from DC's oldest roastery. They also sell breakfast burritos and sandwiches. The breakfast sandwich here isn't what you'd expect – it comes with an egg and meat patty inside a jalapeno and corn muffin. It's one of the top sellers.

Address 65 Massachusetts Avenue NW, Washington DC 20001, +1 (202) 745-7118, www.missionmuffins.org, missionmuffins@missiondc.org // **Getting there** Metro to Union Station (Red Line) // **Hours** Mon–Fri 7–11am // **Ages** 2+

60_MLK MEMORIAL LIBRARY SLIDE

Where a library is also a playground

When you talk too loud in a library, the librarian might ask you to keep your voice down. But not at the Martin Luther King Jr. Memorial Library. There's an amazing surprise here: a secret slide, where you can be as loud as you like. Scream with glee as you slide down from the second to the first floor.

You usually find slides at playgrounds, not libraries, right? So how did this one get here? The answer is simple: parents. When the DC Public Library decided to renovate its central branch, they invited parents with small kids to share what they'd like inside the library. Since there wasn't a place in downtown DC for kids to get their wiggles out, a slide was the winning idea.

The slide is in the Children's Books section. Make sure you spend time browsing picture books, comic books, and novels first. When you're ready, find the secret door leading to the slide. If other kids are there, be sure to take turns. After all, the slide is for everyone to enjoy – even your parents! To go faster, lift up your feet and slide on your bum.

There's plenty to explore at this three-level library. Climb the spiral staircase to the rooftop terrace for benches for reading, native plants, and views of the city. The bottom floor has Marianne's by DC Central Kitchen, a café that provides its workers with job training. Order a hot chocolate or grab a muffin. Throughout the library are exhibits to teach you about DC history and public art, like a piece honoring Martin Luther King Jr., whom the library honors.

TIP: Watch digital art projected onto the walls at nearby CityCenterDC.

Address 901 G Street NW, Washington, DC 20001, +1 (202) 727-0321, www.dclibrary.org/plan-visit/martin-luther-king-jr-memorial-library, firstfloormlk.dcpl@dc.gov // **Getting there** Metro to Metro Center (Blue, Orange, Red, Silver Lines) // **Hours** Mon–Thu 9:30am–9pm, Fri & Sat 9:30am–5:30pm, Sun 1–5pm // **Ages** 2+

61_MONROE STREET MARKET

Balloon art and story time

You can find red tomatoes, balloon art, green cucumbers, and sidewalk chalk at the FRESHFARM Monroe Street Market, the city's most kid-friendly farmers market. Located in the Brookland neighborhood, the market is open every Saturday year-round, and there's usually live music and story time for kids too.

As shoppers wander among the stands of fresh tomatoes and apples grown mere miles from DC, kids gather around the market's main attraction: Chubzy the Clown. The popular clown doesn't just juggle. He's known to make balloon art, including dogs, swords, and many other creations. You can ask Chubzy to make your favorite animal out of balloons.

The Monroe Street Market sets up along a pedestrian-only walkway. So there are no cars nearby, and kids are safe to do a little bit of exploring on their own while the adults pick up tasty things to eat during the coming week. You can smell the scents of fresh fruits, vegetables, and herbs, like peaches and fresh mint. Strawberries, blackberries, and mushrooms are just a few goodies you'll find here. Some farmers let you taste samples!

Farmers markets have a very long history. People have shopped for their food in markets for centuries. Today, DC keeps the tradition alive with dozens of farmers markets all over town. More than carrots, green beans, strawberries, and raspberries, several stands sell goodies popular among children, like empanadas from DMV Empanadas or Filipino doughnuts from Cocoi's Sweets & Pastries. Be sure to try its purple ube doughnut.

Address 716 Monroe Street NE, Washington, DC 20017, www.freshfarm.org/markets/monroe-st // **Getting there** Metro to Brookland-CUA (Red Line) // **Hours** Sat 9am–1pm // **Ages** 0+

TIP: FRESHFARM Dupont Circle Market offers fresh produce and music on Sunday mornings.

62_MOONSHOT STUDIO

Create art for free

At Moonshot Studios, you won't make *papier-mâché* or pottery like you might in your school art class. Rather than crayons, you'll find paint pens. Instead of drawing, you'll create flipbooks. In this studio at the Kennedy Center's THE REACH, you can make art that you can't make anywhere else, and it's all free.

Open every weekend to anyone who wants to create art, Moonshot Studio centers its art projects around themes. During the 50th anniversary of hip-hop music, for example, it set up a real DJ controller for you to play tunes to set the vibe. A giant canvas was set up for kids to do graffiti. After learning more about the history of hip-hop, kids created their very own raps.

TIP: Find the nearby gilded horse sculptures *The Arts of War* and *The Arts of Peace.*

With wonderful performances and concerts, the Kennedy Center is an elevated experience. THE REACH opened in 2019 as a place where anyone can create, be inspired, and connect with others. You don't have to dress up to come here like you might at the Kennedy Center. Come as you are.

The Kennedy Center for the Performing Arts is a living tribute to President John F. Kennedy. Every May, the entire Kennedy Center and THE REACH celebrates his birthday month.

On weekends, you can stop by the Moonshot Studio to create a miniature boat using all kinds of material. Then head to the nearby Reflecting Pool to see if your boat will float. If it sinks, don't worry. Just go back to Moonshot Studio, where it's all about learning, and try again.

Address 2700 F Street NW, Washington, DC 20037, +1 (202) 416 -8000, www.kennedy-center.org/reach/moonshot-studio // **Getting there** Metro to Foggy Bottom-GWU (Blue, Orange, Silver Lines) // **Hours** Moonshot Studio: Sat & Sun 11am–4:30pm; Kennedy Center: daily 10am–midnight // **Ages** 5+

JUSTICE
FOR ALL

63_MUNICIPAL FISH MARKET

Fresh seafood at an old market

You can smell the Municipal Fish Market before you see it, but don't let that scare you away. Opened in 1805, it's the country's oldest, continuously operating, open-air fish market. Depending on the season, you'll find fresh seafood from the area, like crabs in the summer and oysters in the winter.

A number of vendors sell their goods from a barge, a flat-bottomed boat that rises and falls with the tides. So the vendors will be at different levels depending on when you go. At high tide, the barges are higher than you. At low tide, vendors have to lift your seafood up to you.

The largest vendor is Jessie Taylor Seafood, a family-owned business since 1939 that once only sold fresh seafood from the nearby Chesapeake Bay. Today, it's owned by the third generation, and you can find seafood from up and down the East Coast. During hot months, Maryland blue crab is local. During the winter, the crabs migrate south to warmer waters off the coasts of North Carolina and Louisiana, where they're caught and brought to the Municipal Fish Market.

Most of the seafood is kept cold on beds of ice, including octopus, squid, clams, and mussels. But the crabs are alive – you can watch them crawling around. You can tell a crab's gender by the color of its claws. Males' claws are blue, and females' claws have what looks like red nail polish.

Jessie Taylor also sells prepared crab meat to eat right away, four kinds of seafood soup, like cream of crab and clam chowder, and steamed crawfish. Ask for a sample to taste!

TIP: One of the city's cheapest yet very tasty meals is at nearby Falafel Inc.

Address 1100 Maine Avenue SW, Washington, DC 20024, +1 (202) 554-4173, www.wharfdc.com/fish-market // Getting there Metro to L'Enfant Plaza (Blue, Green, Orange, Silver, Yellow Lines) // Hours Mon–Thu 10am–8pm, Fri 9am–8pm, Sat & Sun 8am–8pm // Ages 0+

64_MUSICAL CROSSROADS

Dance to cultural icons

Sometimes, museums are quiet spaces. Hushed voices, slow steps – they can feel very serious. But not at the National Museum of African American History and Culture's Musical Crossroads. Here, quiet doesn't exist. Music of all kinds fills the space. Visitors dance, sing, and recall musical memories.

Musical Crossroads is an interactive exhibit that tells the story of African American music, from the tunes sung during enslavement to the songs that win Grammy Awards today – and everything in between. Before you find the Neighborhood Record Store with a digital table that plays dozens of songs, there's much to know about African American music. Africans from many different cultures were forcibly brought to the United States, which was once a land of oppression. For enslaved people, music became a tool to fight injustice, which continued under segregation. Music became a vehicle for expression and freedom.

Therefore, everything inside Musical Crossroads has deeper meaning. The Neighborhood Record Store isn't just a place to listen to your favorite musician. It represents a safe space, like during segregation in Black neighborhoods, when local record stores were indeed safe, communal places.

While you celebrate African American music, take the time to find some of the exhibit's iconic items: Whitney Houston's Soul Train Award, Marian Anderson's outfit from her 1939 Lincoln Memorial concert, and even Flavor Flav's clock. Plus enjoy learning about the rich history of African Americans.

Address 1400 Constitution Avenue NW, Washington, DC 20560, +1 (844) 750-3012, nmaahc.si.edu/explore/exhibitions/musical-crossroads, nmaahcinfo@si.edu // **Getting there** Metro to Federal Triangle (Blue, Orange, Silver Lines) // **Hours** Mon noon–5:30pm, Tue–Sun 10am–5:30pm // **Ages** 0+

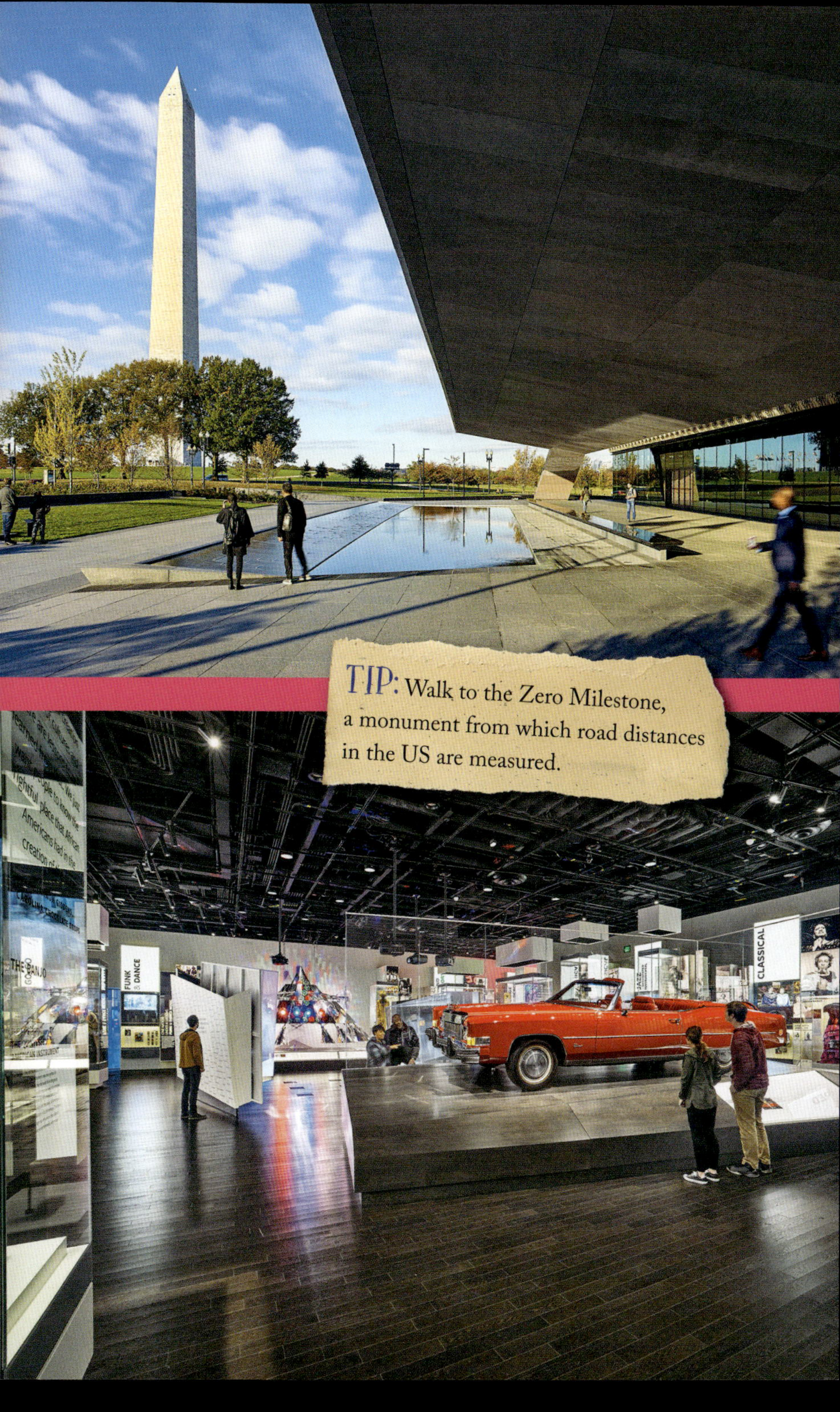

TIP: Walk to the Zero Milestone, a monument from which road distances in the US are measured.

65_NATIONAL BUILDING MUSEUM

Lose time in a grand museum

cool

One of the grandest museums in DC is the National Building Museum, a space dedicated to architecture and design. It might sound like it's more for adults, but it happens to be very appealing to kids, too.

The wonder starts in the Great Hall. Accessible even without a ticket, the Great Hall is one of the largest indoor open spaces to run around. There's a fountain in the middle and grand columns that seem to reach into the sky. The building isn't just a beautiful space – it's historic. It opened in 1887, 22 years after the Civil War ended, as the US Pension Building to help soldiers recover from the war. It became the National Building Museum in 1985.

After getting your wiggles out in the Great Hall, explore the rest of the museum. Start at the "Building Stories" exhibit. With a giant alphabet wall, reading nooks, digital stories projected onto walls, and interactive games, this exhibit explores the architecture and design found in over 150 children's books from 28 countries. When you enter the exhibit, grab a sketchbook to collect stamps throughout the exhibit. Pay attention to peepholes and little windows that only kids find.

TIP: Giant lion sculptures grace the National Law Enforcement Officers Memorial across the street.

The fun doesn't end there. Look for old toys, like the original Lincoln Logs and dollhouses from the 1960s in the "Visible Vault" exhibit. Spend hours in the gift shop – you'll find LEGO sets of famous buildings and more. On Thursday mornings, the museum hosts free story times for younger kids, and the books are picked based on the museum's current exhibits.

Address 401 F Street NW, Washington, DC 20001, +1 (202) 272-2448, www.nbm.org, info@nbm.org // **Getting there** Metro to Judiciary Square (Red Line) // **Hours** Thu–Mon 10am–4pm // **Ages** 2+

66_NATIONAL CHILDREN'S MUSEUM

Where learning is fun for all kids

Founded over 50 years ago, the National Children's Museum was created via an act of Congress when politicians thought the capital needed a national institution for kids! It's the only institution in Washington, DC dedicated entirely to children – not certain kids, but *all* kids.

The museum offers sensory-friendly hours with limited tickets in order to create a more quiet and less crowded experience. But even if you can't go during these hours, do still visit. You can request a free "sensory bag" at any time, with headphones to quiet the noise, a fidget spinner, and a weighted snake to wrap around your shoulders or waist to help reduce anxiety. The museum has a quiet zone with books, a private quiet room, and special programs, including sensory-friendly story time.

Every exhibit is focused on teaching you about STEAM (science, technology, engineering, arts, and math). Learn about the weather by creating rain, lightning, and more on an interactive green screen. Get to know how cars work by racing wooden cars on a special track. Test your paper airplane-making skills and see how far your own creation flies. The Tinkerers Studio always has a craft or experiment for you, like creating your own parachute or making art out of recycled materials.

Spend hours climbing through a three-story rope tunnel to reach colorful pods that look like clouds, or step inside a bubble that engulfs your entire body. There's even dedicated space for infants and toddlers to play on padded floors with soft toys.

TIP: Stroll through the Capital Harvest Market on nearby Woodrow Wilson Plaza from May to November.

Address 1300 Pennsylvania Avenue NW, Washington, DC 20004, +1 (202) 844-2486, www.nationalchildrensmuseum.org // **Getting there** Metro to Federal Triangle (Blue, Orange, Silver Lines) // **Hours** Mon & Wed 9:30am–4:30pm, Thu–Sun 9am–6pm // **Ages** 0+

67_NATIONAL FIRE DOG MONUMENT

Some heroes wear fur

Heroes don't always wear capes. Some wear fur, like Sadie, a labrador trained to sniff out how forest fires started. Working with an arson investigator, Sadie figured out the cause of over 1,000 fires in her home state of Colorado. Now Sadie and her human are memorialized in front of a fire station near downtown Washington, DC at the National Fire Dog Monument.

Only one of several statues depicting dogs in DC, the National Fire Dog Monument has an inspiring story. It was created by an artist named Austin Weishel, the youngest sculptor to have a piece of work memorialized in the nation's capital. When he was little, Weishel didn't love school. Reading was hard for him due to his dyslexia. He found confidence in making art. After a visit to a sculpture factory with his grandparents, he started sculpting. When he designed the National Fire Dog Monument, also known as *Ashes to Answers*, he was only 21 years old!

Weishel's childhood dream was to become a firefighter, and he did. In fact, he was working as a fireman while also sculpting. Creating the National Fire Dog Monument combined the two things he loved. "Believe in yourself, and you can do amazing things if you find your passion," he says.

cute

You'll notice that Sadie never takes her eyes off of the firefighter as she awaits her next command. The details on the dog statue are impressive. It looks like a real dog! You can even hug Sadie, but don't expect soft fur. Sadie is all bronze, but she'll still warm your heart.

Address 500 F Street NW, Washington, DC 20001 // Getting there Metro to Judiciary Square (Red Line) // Hours Unrestricted // Ages 2+

TIP: From firefighting to fighting crime, learn to solve a criminal case at the National Law Enforcement Museum.

68_NATIONAL HERB GARDEN

Taste all the delicious plants

The country's largest designed herb garden is in Washington, DC, and it's not just for show. You can smell and even taste herbs from around the world. There's basil that goes on pizza or in spaghetti sauce, and sage, an herb in Thanksgiving stuffing. They can all be found in the National Herb Garden inside the US National Arboretum.

Before you enter the garden, which looks like a skeleton key if you were to see it from an airplane, you'll learn about herbs. More than green leaves you put in food, herbs are any plants that are useful to humans and enhance our lives when we use them in food, drinks, medicine, candles, dyes for clothes, and more. The National Herb Garden has more than 900 types of plants!

Explore the garden, and you'll find cocoa plants used to make chocolate. Look for bayberries, which are used to make candles. Roses are used to make perfumes. Search for a plant called heliotrope. It's purple and low to the ground, so you'll need to look down. Hold its leaves in your hand and rub it gently. Do you see little bubbles coming up on the leaves like bubble wrap? They burst when you run your fingers over them, releasing oil that smells like cherry and vanilla.

Unlike other herb gardens in the city, you can't harvest the herbs here, but you can tear off a little bit to taste. A fun game to play is "find the cilantro," an herb used in salsa and guacamole. Pinch off a leaf and taste it. Some people really love the taste, but others say it tastes like dirt or even soap. What do you think?

Address 3501 New York Avenue NE, Washington, DC 20002, +1 (202) 245-4523, www.usna.usda.gov, USNA.Comments@usda.gov // **Getting there** Bus B2 to Bladensburg Road & Rand Place NE // **Hours** Daily 8am–5pm // **Ages** 2+

TIP: See the perfect, miniature trees at the National Bonsai & Penjing Museum.

69_NATIONAL POSTAL MUSEUM

Start your own stamp collection

Did you know that the very first stamp was created in the United Kingdom in 1840? It was called the "Penny Black" because it cost one penny. Today, it's so rare that it costs a fortune, but you can see one for yourself at the National Postal Museum.

The National Postal Museum is one of the most interactive museums in DC. Inside the city's former Main Post Office, the museum starts with a history of stamps, and they keep it fun. You can see stamps from countries like India and Kenya. Simply pull open sliding drawers filled with old and newer stamps in every color of the rainbow. You can create a stamp collection on digital screens. Once you have your collection, email it to yourself! You are also welcome to take home real stamps from a table covered with hundreds of them. Find one with the first airplane on it or one with the mountains of Colorado. Pick five to take home and start your stamp collection.

Downstairs is where you'll find all kinds of transportation used to deliver mail across the country. Walk inside an old train or hop in the driver's seat of a mail truck. Don't miss "Owney," an adventurous mutt who traveled the country helping to deliver mail. He was the Railway Post Office's unofficial mascot!

You'll become a Post Office expert – test your skills at interactive stations. One game asks you to sort packages by zip code as fast as you can. Another gives you a digital envelope to read and record the zip code. The envelopes come at you faster and faster. Can you keep up?

Address 2 Massachusetts Avenue NE, Washington, DC 20002, +1 (202) 633-5555, postalmuseum.si.edu // Getting there Metro to Union Station (Red Line) // Hours Daily 10am–5:30pm // Ages 2+

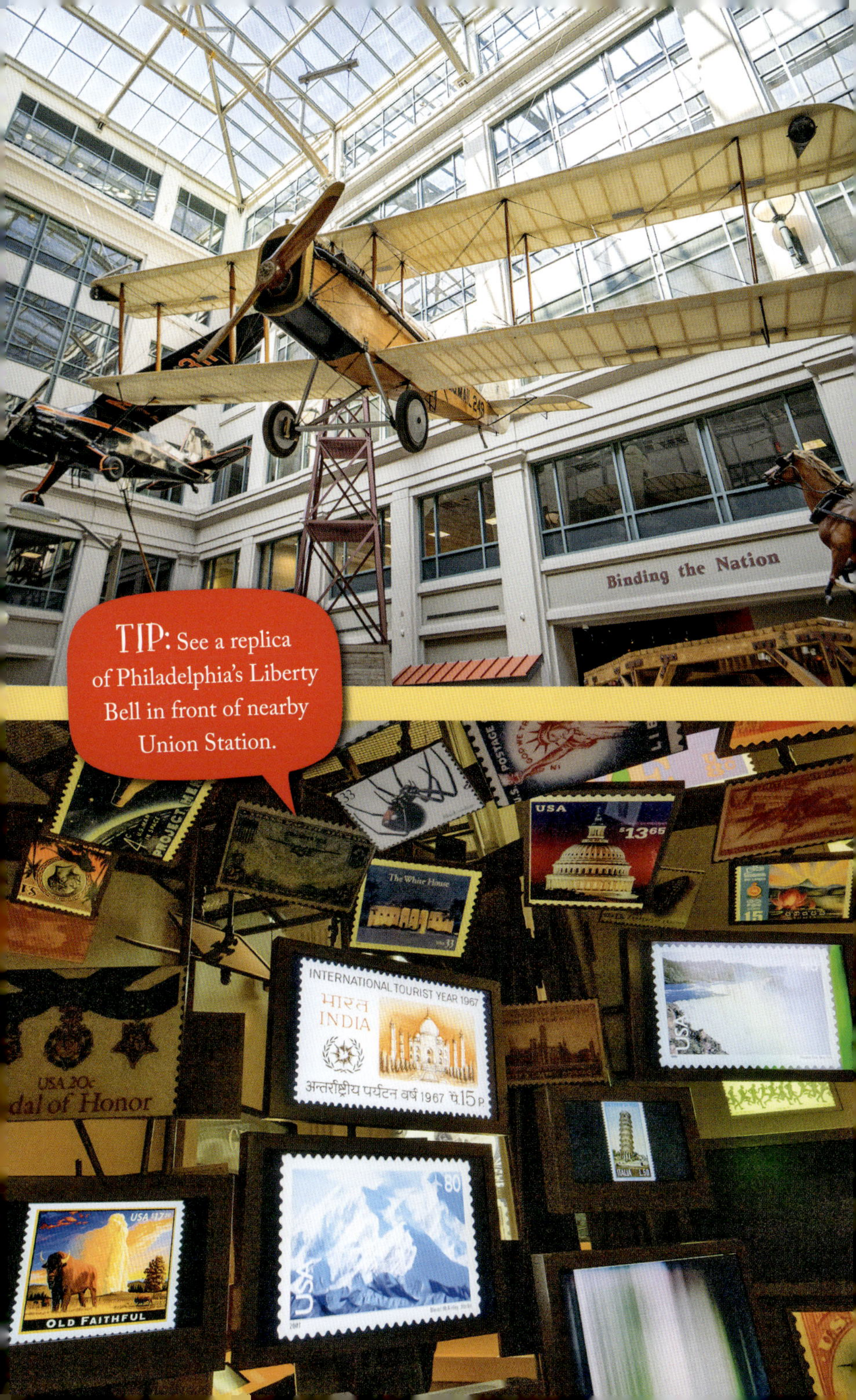

TIP: See a replica of Philadelphia's Liberty Bell in front of nearby Union Station.

70_NATIONALS' FAMILY FUN DAY

Take me out to the ballgame

Imagine this: You just got your jersey signed by a baseball star. After eating a classic hot dog with all the fixings, you're snapping photos with larger-than-life US presidents like George Washington. After the game, you're running the bases of a Major League Baseball stadium as the crowd cheers. This isn't a dream. It's real life at Nationals Park when you visit during their "Family Fundays."

Every Sunday home game at the park, you can create memories that will last a lifetime. Gates open early for ticket holders to enjoy story time, when Nationals players read favorite children's books out loud. You even get to take the book to read at home for free! Before the game, Nationals players will sign autographs on a first-come, first-served basis. Then you can pick up a hot dog, chips, and bottled water for the game. Kids eat for free! You can also go to the play zone near centerfield or ask for a baseball-themed activity book from Guest Services. Sometimes there is face painting and a balloon artist squeaking out colorful dogs and swords.

There's a lot to experience during the game itself, like kid-friendly giveaways of stuffed animals, bobbleheads, and more. In the middle of the fourth inning, giant presidents and mascots race on the field. You can take a photo with them during the fifth inning or before the game. After the game, run the bases with other kids. If it's your first baseball game, don't forget to pick up a "First Game" certificate at Guest Services to remember your incredible day.

Address 1500 South Capitol Street SE, Washington, DC 20003, +1 (202) 675-6287, www.mlb.com/nationals/tickets/specials/family-funday, service@nationals.com // **Getting there** Metro to Navy Yard-Ballpark (Green & Yellow Lines) // **Hours** Fun Days: Sun noon–8pm; see website for Nationals' schedule // **Ages** 4-12

TIP: Catch a Major League Soccer game with DC United at nearby Audi Field.

71_NEWTON APPLE TREE

Play near a science-loving tree

Over 350 years ago in England, Sir Isaac Newton watched an apple fall from a tree. The simple sight would inspire him to think about the world in a new way. If you haven't learned about Sir Isaac Newton in science class yet, you will. He developed the theory of Earth's gravity relative to the moon. And you can impress your science teacher by visiting an actual Newton apple tree.

In the middle of International Park is a clone of the original apple tree that first inspired Newton. It's not fenced off or in a museum. It's right there in a public park, and you can sit beneath it just like Newton did.

How did such an important tree end up in a small park in DC? There's a story. The land that it's on used to be the campus of the National Bureau of Standards (later called the National Institute of Standards and Technology – NIST). Near where the Newton tree is today was a building where scientists continued to study gravity. After visiting the United Kingdom, an NIST scientist asked if it would be possible to bring a Newton apple tree to Washington, and a cutting from the original tree was planted here in 1957. As the years went by, it grew into a big tree. After the first tree in DC died, a new one was planted in 2000. Every fall, crab apples grow on the famous tree. You'll see a plaque that reads, *Science has its traditions as well as its frontiers*. The hope is that the tree will inspire a new generation of scientists to carry on the work of thinking people like Sir Isaac Newton. Don't miss the Greek statue nearby.

TIP: Look at all the flags of the embassies surrounding International Park.

Address 3500 International Drive Northwest, Washington, DC 20008 // **Getting there** Metro to Van Ness-UDC (Red Line) // **Hours** Unrestricted // **Ages** 2+

72_O STREET MANSION

Find over 80 secret doors

The O Street Mansion and Museum is one of the quirkiest places in the city. The five interconnected mansions in Dupont Circle offer over 100 different rooms and 80 secret doors. Most people can only find a handful of the doors!

Built at the end of the 19th century, the mansions have a lot of history and many stories to tell. One of the mansions housed Rosa Parks. During the Civil Rights Movement, Parks, who was Black, bravely sat in a whites-only section of a public bus. Her courage helped lead to a nation where everyone is treated better, regardless of the color of their skin, but it also brought her danger. The mansion was her safe haven.

Today, the O Street Mansion and Museum are part hotel, part museum, and part giant treasure trove. Each room is filled with trinkets, some of which are fragile, so explore carefully. Dolls, guitars, books – every item you see is for sale. Also enjoy brunches, overnight visits, after-hour tours, book discussions, and more.

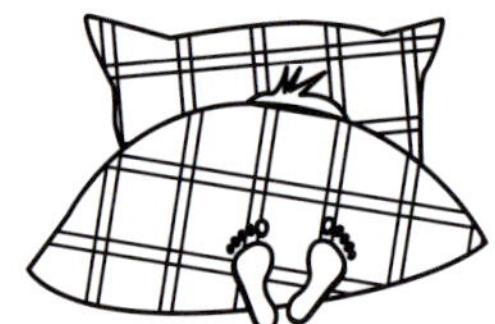

Pay special attention to mirrors – sometimes they open into a hidden room. While hunting for secret doors, find the giant lips that visitors can walk through. Nearby is a pinball machine for playing. Or find the black toilet that's shaped like a piano. Every room is whimsical. There's a Western-themed room with cowboy hats on the bed, and one that's modeled after a log cabin, where logs create a winding staircase. Even the bathroom door is made from logs! You can visit over and over again and always find something new.

TIP: Two blocks away is cash-only Bagels Etc. which serves New York-style bagels, including a chocolate-chip one.

Address 2020 O Street NW, Washington, DC 20036, +1 (202) 496-2070, www.omansion.com // **Getting there** Metro to Dupont Circle (Red Line) // **Hours** Sun–Wed 9am–6pm, Thu–Sat 9am–9pm // **Ages** 5+

73_OLD POST OFFICE PAVILION

See the entire city from up high

Would you like to know one of DC's best-kept secrets? Here you go: The Old Post Office Pavilion has one of the best views of Washington, DC. While many people take the elevator up the Washington Monument to its Observation Deck, the Old Post Office Pavilion has the same views and fewer people. You don't even need a ticket – you can just walk right in!

How did this tall tower come to the capital? It was built in 1899 as a grand post office building. Until 1914, people could drop off mail here to be delivered around the country. Everyone knew the building because it looks like a castle, with all of its spires pointing into the sky. The clock tower has always been one of the tallest structures in the city.

Today, the building is a museum. Walk in any day and take two elevators to the 270-foot observation deck, where you can see for 12 miles across the DC area on a clear day. Spot the US Capitol, The Pentagon across the Potomac River, and even The White House.

Another fact that many people don't realize is that the Old Post Office Pavilion is a bell tower too. Great Britain gave the US Congress the 10 ringing bells in the tower as a bicentennial gift in 1976 celebrating 200 years of the signing of the Declaration of Independence. Originally intended for the US Capitol, the bells are replicas of the ones inside London's Westminster Abbey. The 10 bells ring on federal holidays, special occasions, and every Thursday evening at 7pm, when members of the Washington Ringing Society practice. If you're within four blocks, you'll hear the peals.

TIP: See the original Constitution of the United States at the National Archives.

Address 1100 Pennsylvania Avenue NW, Washington, DC 20004, www.nps.gov/nama/planyourvisit/opot.htm // **Getting there** Metro to Federal Triangle (Blue, Orange, Silver Lines) // **Hours** Daily 9am–5pm // **Ages** 4+

74_ORANGUTAN CROSSING

Watch great apes in the sky at the National Zoo

When you look up at the Smithsonian's National Zoo, you may see orangutans on a tightrope above you. It's a rare sight and one that evokes squeals of delight from visitors. The tightrope is called the O-Line and allows the orangutans who live at the zoo to travel between the Great Ape House and the Think Tank, where zookeepers study the orange primates. The tightrope is 50 feet off the ground and connects to eight towers.

There are only three species of orangutans – Sumatran, Bornean, and Tapanuli – and they only live in two places in the world: on the Pacific islands of Borneo and Sumatra. In fact, orangutans are the only great ape that live on the continent of Asia. They have long fur, eat with their feet, and are the world's heaviest tree-dwelling animals. There aren't many orangutans left on Earth; they are endangered.

The National Zoo is lucky to have seven of them, but only six walk the O-Line. Lucy, the oldest orangutan at the zoo at 50 years old, has never tried to walk it. Red makes up for it. Red was born at the zoo and learned how to walk the O-Line from his mom. He now does backflips, somersaults, and other acrobatics on the O-Line.

Orangutans are their own animals. Sometimes they sit on the O-Line for a long time. There are times when they have to go potty while sitting on the tightrope, but don't worry. Zookeepers keep a close eye and block off the pedestrian walkway, so no one gets dirty. Within minutes, the path is cleaned, and giggling visitors continue their visit.

Address 3001 Connecticut Avenue NW, Washington, DC 20008, +1 (202) 633-4888, www.nationalzoo.si.edu // Getting there Metro to Woodley Park-Zoo/Adams Morgan (Red Line) // Hours Daily 8am–4pm // Ages 1+

TIP: See animals you can pet at Crumbs & Whiskers, a cat café.

75_OUTDOOR SKATING PAVILION

Rolling and rocking in Anacostia

Tucked away in the 1,200-acre Anacostia National Park is the Skating Pavilion, the city's only outdoor skating pavilion and also the country's only skating pavilion inside a national park. DJs blast music as kids, parents, and grandparents roller skate near the Anacostia River with little care in the world. It's a slice of the city for all of DC's children and adults – and visitors too.

The rink is open year round, and free skate rentals are offered from Memorial Day to Labor Day. One valid ID card can rent pairs for up to five people. Be ready for old-school roller skating on four sturdy wheels, rather than sleek inline skating. And stay for the local DJs. On weekend evenings, they'll play go-go tunes, DC's official music, which was born just a few miles from here. It's a type of funk music, and its songs are easy to follow and beats fun to dance to, even if you don't know the words.

All experience levels are welcome to skate here. If you're new to skating, you can practice and learn the ropes with the help of free skating aids. Often, more experienced skaters will also lend a hand to younger skaters by teaching basic skating skills.

The skating pavilion comes with lots of flare. Many regular skaters like to dress in shiny clothes, and sometimes they wear skates that light up as they glide across the floor. They're talented too. You'll see experienced skaters skating backwards and spinning in the air. So even if you don't want to skate, you can always enjoy the show from the sidelines.

Address 1500 Anacostia Drive SE, Washington, DC 20020, +1 (202) 692-6080, www.nps.gov/anac/planyourvisit/roller-skating.htm // **Getting there** Metro to Potomac Avenue (Blue, Orange, Silver Lines) // **Hours** Rink: Memorial Day–Labor Day daily 6am–10pm; Park: unrestricted // **Ages** 4+

TIP: Next door is a giant map of the US with boulders representing the Rocky Mountains.

76_THE PEOPLE'S HOUSE

Pretend you're the President

Not everyone can visit The White House. You have to get tickets months in advance from your Representative in the US Congress, and often no tickets are available. You can see the presidential house from the outside, but it's special to walk its halls. Now you can have that experience regardless, thanks to The People's House: A White House Experience just across the street!

The People's House is a recreation of The White House for all to visit. Inside is the city's only replica of the Oval Office, where the President takes phone calls and does work. Relax on replica Oval Office couches, where world leaders and very important people have sat over the decades. Sit at the President's desk and make some calls of your own. For smaller kids, there's even a trapdoor under the President's desk to crawl through like President Kennedy's kids did.

The entire experience is hands-on. There's an immersive theater that transforms into different White House rooms. Touch the walls to unlock fun facts. Sit at the table in the Cabinet Room and pretend to make important decisions that affect the country and world. In the "People's Voices" exhibit, you'll meet permanent White House staff, like housekeepers and butlers. You can even take a photo of yourself digitally placed on The White House balcony.

TIP: Lay on a carpet and gaze up at a colorful art installation at the nearby Renwick Gallery.

First Lady Jackie Kennedy is to thank for The People's Experience. It's run by The White House Historical Association, an organization she started to deepen the public's connection to this very important house.

Address 1700 Pennsylvania Avenue NW, Washington, DC 20006, +1 (771) 888-4007, www.thepeopleshouse.org, thepeopleshouse@whha.org // **Getting there** Metro to Farragut North (Red Line) // **Hours** Daily 9am–5pm // **Ages** 2+

77_PLANET WORD'S RESTROOMS

A museum where every room is fun

"I stink, ...

Inside the small, historic Franklin School, Planet Word is an interactive museum about language and words, with fun exhibits about how the English language came to be, words in different languages, poetry, and more. The restrooms here have been voted among the country's best because they tell jokes. And inside the second floor's public restrooms are funny, potty-mouthed phrases on the walls. Many are inspired by playwright William Shakespeare, like "Farting is such sweet sorrow," and "To pee or not to pee, that is the question." "I stink, therefore I am" is a riff off of mathematician René Descartes' famous philosophical quote.

... therefore I am."

Learn about music lyrics at the karaoke station, and sing to your favorite artists, like Taylor Swift, and songs from movies like *Moana*. Snap photos with a friend at the photo booth, where you'll pose with words like "Ravishing" and "Ostentatious." Laugh at the joke stations or try a word-focused escape room at Lexicon Lane. And visit the library, where books literally come to life – there's even a secret poetry room. Can you find it?

Be sure to check out the unique restrooms on every floor of the museum. The walls in the ones on the lower floors are inscribed with the word "bathroom" in different languages: *baño* in Spanish, *badezimmer* in German, and *les toilettes* in French. Head to the third-floor toilets to learn how to say, "Where is the bathroom?" in Mandarin, Arabic, and many other languages. If you need a translation, simply scan the QR code.

TIP: Learn about local history through interactive exhibits at the DC History Center.

If at first you don't succeed, flush, flush again.

Address 925 13th Street NW, Washington, DC 20005, +1 (202) 931-3139, www.planetwordmuseum.org, connect@planetwordmuseum.org // **Getting there** Metro to McPherson Square (Blue, Orange, Silver Lines) // **Hours** Mon & Wed–Fri 10am–5pm, Sat & Sun 10am–6pm // **Ages** 4+

78_PLASTIC BOTTLE CAP MURALS

Help save the planet through art

Down an alley in a neighborhood called Tenleytown are murals made from plastic bottle caps. Along the fence of Karen Lash's house, the murals are meant to help educate us on plastics. Contrary to popular opinion, many plastics are not recyclable. They last pretty much forever, and many are made with chemicals that aren't good for the environment. These facts are the inspiration behind Lash's murals.

After listening to a report on National Public Radio about the effects of plastics filling Earth's oceans and seas, Lash set out on a mission to inspire people to use less plastic. She collected plastic bottle caps and created the murals in her alleyway. Look for a rainbow, a "Tree of Life," and a red, white, and blue mural that reads, "Vote." Lash also included a few "Easter eggs" in the murals, like a portrait of the late Supreme Court Justice Ruth Bader Ginsburg and a rubber duck covered in "recycle" symbols.

Also along the fence is information about the dangers of plastics and how we can help reduce their use. One tip is to buy products in non-plastic containers. Another is to buy used items rather than new ones. You can also buy food in bulk rather than in single packages that use more plastic. Forgo plastic cutlery with your take-out and use a metal fork from home.

Lash's alleyway is in a residential part of town, and the wide alley welcomes dog walkers, kids on bicycles, and neighbors taking a stroll. Sometimes she puts out a bucket for bottle cap donations to add to her murals.

TIP: There's an old building that looks like a castle in Fort Reno Park close by.

Address Alley in between 44th & 45th Streets NW and Burlington Place & Chesapeake Street NW // Getting there Metro to Tenleytown (Red Line) // Hours Unrestricted // Ages 3+

79_THE PUZZLE POST

Borrow a jigsaw puzzle

When you just want to stay home and relax, first stop by the Puzzle Post in the front yard of a Capitol Hill rowhouse. Inside the three Little Free Library boxes and a repurposed newspaper stand are dozens of jigsaw puzzles for anyone to borrow. Sometimes you'll find puzzles of pictures of world wonders, like the Taj Mahal in India or Machu Picchu in Peru. At other times, there are puzzles of scenes from Disney movies like *Toy Story* or *The Lion King*. There are easier puzzles with 100 pieces and more challenging ones with 1,000 pieces. There's a puzzle for almost everyone!

The person behind the Puzzle Post is a woman named SuzAnne. During the pandemic, she started doing puzzles to help pass time at home. Rather than have them pile up inside her home, she created a Little Free Library as a gift to her neighborhood. Within days, puzzle donations poured in as her neighbors dropped off the puzzles they'd finished. There were so many donations that she added two more boxes to hold them all.

Today, anyone can take, borrow, swap, or donate jigsaw puzzles. If you take a puzzle and notice a missing piece, let SuzAnne know. She makes replacement pieces. At first, she used a 3D printer to create the replacements, but now she creates a mold, and just hours later, the puzzles are complete again!

TIP: Two blocks away is The Pretzel Bakery, the city's only bakery of its kind.

The Puzzle Post is open all the time, and there are always new puzzles in the boxes. People from other neighborhoods drop off used puzzles, and there's even a puzzle club that contributes regularly.

Address 1306 C Street SE, Washington, DC 20003 // **Getting there** Metro to Eastern Market (Blue, Orange, Silver Lines) // **Hours** Unrestricted // **Ages** 5+

80_RIVER HORSE STATUE

Pet a hippo

There are more statues in Washington, DC than you can count. US Presidents, Civil War Union Generals, Civil Rights activists – it's hard to keep track of them all. Among the sea of statues are a few funny ones, like the *River Horse Statue* on the campus of George Washington University. A river horse is a hippo! The name hippopotamus comes from the Greek words "hippo" meaning horse and "potamus" meaning river. Unlike the hippos at the National Zoo, this is one you can pet!

The *River Horse Statue* is an unusual sight on the university campus named after the country's first president. How did it wind up here? It's a funny story. In 1996, the university's then-president saw the statue of a hippo at a flea market. He thought it would make a good gift for his wife. She didn't agree. She refused the gift, and so the president gave it to George Washington University's Class of 2000 instead. Today, it's the university's unofficial mascot. Students often rub the nose of the hippo as they walk by, and some even dress up as hippos at sporting events.

When you visit the *River Horse Statue*, you'll find a plaque with a story about how George and Martha Washington used to watch hippos bathe in the Potomac River. Don't worry. This is obviously not true. Hippos don't live in the wild in the US and never have. But they did live at The White House… kind of. President Calvin Coolidge was given a Liberian pygmy hippo named Billy, but he went straight to the National Zoo and was the most popular animal there.

Address 730 21st Street NW, Washington, DC 20052 // **Getting there** Metro to Foggy Bottom-GWU (Blue, Orange, Silver Lines) // **Hours** Unrestricted // **Ages** 2+

TIP: See ancient rugs and cloth at the nearby Textile Museum.

81_ROCK CREEK PLANETARIUM

Gaze at the stars above the city

The North Star and the Big Dipper are just a few stars you'll find in the night sky. One of the best ways to see them without staying up late is at a planetarium, a large dome-shaped theater that projects the night's sky onto the inside dome, creating an experience that's better than going to the movies. Sit back in one of the comfy seats and learn about the wonders and sparkles in space. The Planetarium at Rock Creek Park is the only planetarium within the National Park Service.

How did a planetarium end up in a national park surrounded by trees? After lobbying by a group of astronomers for more education about space, the Planetarium at Rock Creek Park opened in 1960, nine years before Neil Armstrong and Buzz Aldrin became the first humans to set foot on the moon. Ever since, family-friendly programs have run to connect all to the wonder of space.

Throughout the year, you can watch different films created especially for planetariums about galaxies far from Earth. One year, for example, the featured planetarium film was about how different generations of Indigenous societies around the world see the sky. Not only did you walk away with more knowledge about space, but you understood different cultures and countries.

No matter what experience is projected onto the planetarium dome, you may very well leave with an inspiration to become an astronaut. The planetarium is inside a nature center, so make sure you visit the exhibit about native plants and wildlife that live in Rock Creek Park.

Address 5200 Glover Road NW, Washington, DC 20015, +1 (202) 895-6070, www.nps.gov/rocr/planyourvisit/planetarium.htm // **Getting there** Bus C81, C87 to Military Road & Oregon Avenue NW // **Hours** Thu–Sun 9am–5pm // **Ages** 4+

TIP: Visit the only other planetarium in DC at the Smithsonian Air and Space Museum.

82_ROCK CREEK TENNIS CENTER

Learn to serve where the greats have played

It's not every day that you can learn how to play tennis on courts where international stars like Serena Williams and Roger Federer have played. Every year, tennis greats descend upon Washington, DC to compete at the Washington Open at the Rock Creek Tennis Center. When it's not used for professional tennis tournaments, though, it's a place where anyone can learn and play tennis. Classes and leagues for kids five years old and up are offered on over two dozen indoor and outdoor courts.

Tennis today is played with rackets, but it didn't start out that way. French monks in the 12th century first played a version of tennis where they hit the ball back and forth with their hands. When you go to the Rock Creek Tennis Center, first try hitting the ball with your hands. It's hard! Those French monks must have been strong. Luckily, the monks put on gloves to reduce the pain. It wasn't until 400 years later that rackets were used, probably a relief to a lot of French monks. Modern tennis took form in England, which is still home to Wimbledon, the most famous tennis tournament.

Rock Creek Tennis Center is the place to learn tennis in the city. Its junior program teaches kids as young as five how to play! Sign up for classes or reserve a court for practice. For a more unusual experience, learn to play inside the bubble. It looks like a giant marshmallow. It makes the experience more magical. For younger kids, there's a playground nearby and shaded picnic tables. Bring a packed lunch or snacks!

TIP: You can also play tennis at Rose Park, where tennis stars Margaret and Matilda Roumania Peters played.

Address 5220 16th Street NW, Washington, DC 20011, +1 (202) 722-5949, www.rockcreektennis.com/lessons/junior-programs // **Getting there** Bus S2 to 16th & Kennedy Streets NW // **Hours** See website for schedule // **Ages** 5+

83_ROOSEVELT ISLAND

A presidential memorial in the Potomac River

When you need a break from the hustle and bustle of city life, go spend some time enjoying this pedestrian-only island in the Potomac River. You may be able to see the Georgetown skyline, but you're far from the city when you're on this island. It's actually closer to Arlington, Virginia, but the island is technically in Washington, DC and comes with a long history.

Before Europeans settled throughout the area, the native Nacotchtank people lived on the island. Decades later, a man named John Mason built a mansion and a farm here and used enslaved people to harvest his crops. But Roosevelt Island's story doesn't end there. This island where people were once held in slavery would later be used as a training camp for the US Colored Troops during the Civil War. Soldiers fighting for their very freedom were trained in battle here.

In the 1930s, Roosevelt Island became a shrine to the 26th President Theodore Roosevelt, known for his expansion of the National Parks – he created five new national parks during his presidency. He loved the outdoors so much that he's known as the "conservation president."

So it's only appropriate then that Roosevelt Island is a wooded space with trails for the public to enjoy. You can spot wildlife, like turtles and birds of all kinds, along the trail. In the center of the island is an impressive memorial to President Roosevelt, with a larger-than-life statue of him and a network of fountains throughout. The northernmost path offers a nice view of Georgetown.

Address Theodore Roosevelt Island Park, Washington, DC 20001, +1 (703) 289-2500, www.nps.gov/this/index.htm // Getting there Metro to Rosslyn (Blue, Orange, Silver Lines) // Hours Daily 6am–10pm // Ages 2+

THEODORE
ROOSEVELT
TIP: You can also explore Columbia Island in the Potomac River.

84_ROTUNDA OF THE PROVINCES

Exploring at the Canadian Embassy

To hear your echo, stand in the middle of the Embassy of Canada's Rotunda of the Provinces, a tall structure with pillars and a dome. Take turns standing in the spot and say your name out loud. Or squeeze in with your friends and sing your favorite song. The echo turns it into a unique melody.

The Rotunda of the Provinces is part of the Embassy of Canada, which sits just a few blocks from the US Capitol on the famous Pennsylvania Avenue NW, where US presidents walk for every inauguration and where large marches take place. When the embassy opened in 1989, it was one of the few embassies in DC that was not behind big gates. So anyone can explore the grounds here.

An architect named Arthur Erickson from the Canadian province of British Columbia designed the embassy, one of the largest in DC. He built the Rotunda of the Provinces with 12 big pillars representing the number of Canadian provinces and territories in 1989. Nunavut became its own territory 10 years later, and its crest is honored inside the rotunda.

Just after US Thanksgiving (Canada celebrates its own Thanksgiving on a different day), a Christmas tree from Canada's Nova Scotia is placed in the middle of the rotunda. On the lower rotunda level is a waterfall where you can get your hands wet. Find the huge *Spirit of Haida Gwaii* statue that is depicted on the Canadian $20 bill. And visit the gallery inside the embassy, which features works by Canadian artists. It's open to the public and rotates exhibits regularly.

Address 501 Pennsylvania Avenue NW, Washington, DC 20001, +1 (202) 682-1740 // **Getting there** Metro to Archives-Navy Memorial-Penn Quarter (Green & Yellow Lines) // **Hours** Unrestricted, viewable from the outside only // **Ages** 2+

TIP: Find The Chess Players statue by Lloyd Lillie in nearby John Marshall Park.

85_SAINT ELIZABETHS CAMPUS

Learn history through ruins of an old hospital

Though some say that the 300-acre campus of Saint Elizabeths is haunted, you probably won't find ghosts here. But you will learn history. Wander the east side of the campus, and you'll find old, red-brick buildings waiting for repairs. Their walls tell many tales.

Saint Elizabeths was once the country's first federally funded hospital for those suffering from mental illness. When it opened in the middle of the 19th century, it was revolutionary. Unlike other overcrowded mental health institutions, Saint Elizabeths had a private room for every patient. It sat on a hill by the Anacostia River, offering views of nature. The idea was that a beautiful setting would help heal the mind.

However, it wasn't all so nice. Doctors at Saint Elizabeths would treat patients badly. Sometimes they used electroshock therapy, sending electric shocks throughout patient's bodies, and other scary treatments. Because of these horrors, some say the campus is haunted. Two historic cemeteries still exist on the campus and help tell stories of former patients.

Saint Elizabeths is no longer a mental health institution. The Department of Homeland Security uses the west side of the campus, while the east side is being redeveloped for the public. There's a playground, a seasonal farmers market, and even the Entertainment & Sports Arena where the Mystics, DC's women's professional basketball team, play. On occasion, the US General Services offers tours of the west side of the campus.

Address 1100 Oak Drive SE, Washington, DC 20032, www.stelizabethsdevelopment.com // Getting there Metro to Congress Heights (Green Line) // Hours Unrestricted // Ages 3+

TIP: Watch the Mystics, DC's women's basketball team, play at CareFirst Arena.

86_SATURDAY MORNING LIVE

Performing arts for kids in a beautiful theater

Puppet shows, story time, music, dance – there's something for everyone at *Saturday Morning Live!* at the National Theatre, two blocks from The White House.

Every month, the country's second-oldest, continuously operating theater opens its doors to children and their families for free performances. A tradition since 1980, *Saturday Morning Live!* hosts two performances monthly from September to June. Often they are themed. During November's National Native American Heritage Month, Dovie Thomason, award-winning Native storyteller, might read children's books about the Earth. Children dance to and play with Latin American instruments during October's Hispanic American Heritage Month.

There's more to see at the theater than just the performances of *Saturday Morning Live!* When you walk into the historic theater, you'll pass large posters of famous performances, like *Cats* and *Les Misérables*. Walk up the carpeted stairs to find a table with coloring pages and crayons. You can take a sheet and color during the performances. Nearby is a backdrop for photos to remember the time you visited a fancy theater.

Many of the performers are local to DC, and they keep the programs short, between 30 and 45 minutes, so that kids can pay close attention. And lots of the experiences are interactive. If an author is reading her book, for example, you can ask a question in the middle of story time. Sometimes, you can even go onto the theater's main stage and be the main character.

Address 1321 Pennsylvania Avenue NW, Washington, DC 20004, +1 (202) 783-3370, www.nationaltheatre.org/saturday-morning-live, information@nationaltheatre.org // **Getting there** Metro to Federal Triangle (Blue, Orange, Silver Lines) // **Hours** See website for seasonal schedule // **Ages** 3–6

TIP: Inlaid on Freedom Plaza is part of the original 1791 map of Washington, DC.

87_SCULPTURE GARDEN ICE RINK

Skate among museums

Snowflakes gently fall from the sky as ice skaters glide along with a backdrop of the National Archives. It feels like a scene in a holiday movie, but it's real life in the capital city.

For decades, tourists and locals have met on an inch-thick ice skating rink surrounded by sculptures and museums within the National Gallery of Art campus. Open mid-November to mid-March, the National Gallery of Art Sculpture Garden Ice Rink is bigger than the famous one at Rockefeller Center in New York City, and it welcomes visitors every day of the week. There's nothing quite like skating among iconic museums when they're lit up at night.

There's a nominal fee for skating and skate rentals, and you can bring your own skates if you like. Each ticket is good for two 45-minute sessions. (The rink gets resurfaced every hour for 15 minutes to make sure it's always smooth for all.) You can also take skating lessons if you sign up in advance.

TIP: Take a spin on the nearby old-fashioned carousel on the National Mall.

After your time on the ice, walk a few steps to the Pavillion Café and warm up with a cup of hot chocolate or hot cider and snacks. Then explore the Sculpture Garden's 20+ different works of art. Look for *Spider* by artist Louise Bourgeois, the yellow *House 1* by Roy Lichtenstein, and *Thinker on a Rock* by Barry Flanagan. Some of the sculptures are hidden, so look hard! Extra points for finding the word "Amor," or Love in Spanish.

No matter the season, there's always something to see in the Sculpture Garden. The ice rink becomes a grand fountain – you may enjoy refreshing your feet in the cool water on hot days.

Address 7th Street & Constitution Avenue NW, Washington, DC 20565, www.nga.gov/skating // **Getting there** Metro to Archives-Navy Memorial-Penn Quarter (Green & Yellow Lines) // **Hours** Skating rink: mid-November–mid-March, Sun–Thu 11am–9pm, Fri & Sat 11am–11pm // **Ages** 3+

88_SIDEWALK SOLAR SYSTEM

Jump from planet to planet

When you look up at the sky at night, you can see so much more in the solar system than stars. Did you know that almost 200 different moons have been found in our solar system? Or that out of the eight planets, Venus is the hottest? Including Earth, eight planets orbit around our Sun, and a fun way to study them all is to visit the American Geophysical Union.

The AGU is all about Earth and space science, and bringing science to the public in fun, educational, and inspiring ways. It believes in that mission so much that it added the sidewalk solar system for everyone to enjoy. Each planet reflects the size and distance relative to the other planets. For example, you'll notice that Saturn is much bigger than Earth. The designers thought of every detail. Material in the sidewalk solar system sparkles at night when light from streetlights hits it. The effect looks like stars flickering.

Once you're done studying the planets, look up at the American Geophysical Union's building. In a city filled with office buildings, this one stands out. It's designed to look like the helm of a ship, as if the geophysicists here are sailing through the city. Another interesting tidbit about the building is that it's the first net-zero building in DC. That means they only consume energy that they renew. Right under the solar system is the wet well that turns waste water into energy to heat and cool the building. You can book a free tour online and can go see inside their building too!

Address 2000 Florida Avenue NW, Washington, DC 20009, +1 (202) 462-6900, www.agu.org/building/pages/tour // **Getting there** Metro to Dupont Circle (Red Line) // **Hours** Unrestricted from the outside; register online for tours // **Ages** 3+

TIP: Visit the Family Gallery inside The Phillips Collection, the country's first modern art museum.

89_SOUTHWEST DUCK POND

Feed ducks in an urban oasis

Shade is hard to come by during the hot DC summers. But if you find yourself sweating in the humidity, don't despair. In the Southwest Waterfront neighborhood is an urban oasis called the Southwest Duck Pond. Large trees shade the block-long park. Bring peas and halved grapes, or other food that's safe to feed the ducks that are often found in the pond, or relax in one of the many red rocking chairs by the water.

Within one of the city's most historic neighborhoods and surrounded by award-winning architecture, the Southwest Duck Pond is a local institution. Created in the 1970s as a park for local residents, it remains a place where neighbors can connect. The annual Duck Pond Party includes local musicians, art, family-friendly games, and duck-friendly snacks. The Fishing Derby, one of the most beloved events here, takes place on the first Saturday of June. Dozens of fish are released into the pond, and fishing rods and bait are provided for all who want to learn how to fish.

Even if there's no event going on at the park, you will still enjoy your visit. Among the shaded pond's peninsulas and rocking chairs is a three-story Little Free Library filled with dozens of books, as well as the SW DC Tiny Toy Exchange box. It's filled with toys – find one you like, and you can take it home. There's also colorful art throughout and around the park.

This peaceful spot connects you to nature right in the middle of a major city. It's a quiet space to escape and find much-needed summer shade.

Address 520 I Street SW, Washington, DC 20024 // Getting there Metro to Waterfront (Green Line) // Hours Unrestricted // Ages 1+

TIP: Southwest Library hosts regular story time, playtime, and movies.

90_SPACE FOR EARTH

Dance with stars and planets

You can't go to space yet, but you can visit the National Air and Space Agency (NASA). Inside the Mary W. Jackson NASA Headquarters' West Lobby is the Earth Information Center. Thanks to NASA and other agencies, information about our planet and climate change can be transmitted from space, and you can interact with that information in fun ways here.

The most popular exhibit is "Space for Earth." Walk through an LED light tunnel, and you'll enter a black box. Within seconds, an interactive film about Earth's weather and climate projects onto the walls. As you learn about rain patterns, you can play and dance in the digital rain and splash in digital puddles. Swing one arm, and the rain bounces right off.

After the roughly seven-minute, immersive experience, explore the rest of the Earth Information Center. "Earth Pulse" is a large, chandelier-like sculpture that lights up. When the lights travel up, that means information is being transmitted from Earth to the International Space Station. When the lights shoot down, information is being sent back to Earth. A large screen and touch stations invite visitors to explore the data we have about our planet, like how clean our air is and how much water we have.

Walk outside to the East Lobby to find a replica space suit, a real moon rock that you can touch, and a café that sells space-themed pastries and drinks. The gift shop sells plush aliens, space costumes, solar system models, space ice cream, and other space-themed toys.

Address 300 E Street SW, East Lobby, Washington, DC 20546, +1 (202) 358-0000, www.earth.gov/stories/immersive_earth // **Getting there** Metro to L'Enfant Plaza (Blue, Green, Orange, Silver, Yellow Lines) // **Hours** Mon–Fri 8:30am–5:30pm // **Ages** 4+

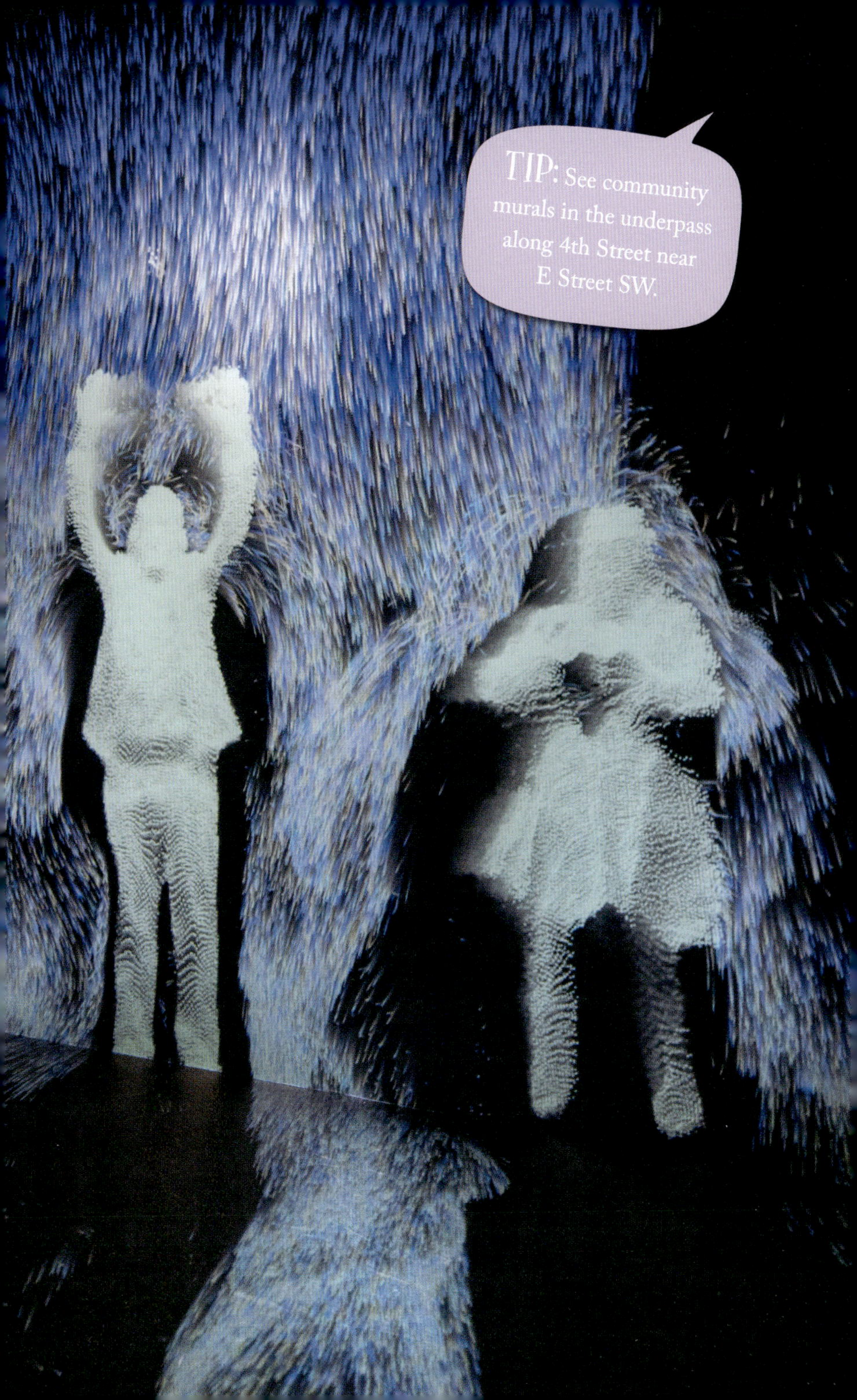
TIP: See community murals in the underpass along 4th Street near E Street SW.

91_THE SPACE WINDOW

An actual moon rock at the National Cathedral

There are many beautiful and special stained glass windows in the National Cathedral, the second largest church in the country. The *Space Window* is the most famous one.

Inspired by actual photos, this window looks as if you're staring into space. Among the multiple circles in the design is a red one. In its center is a sliver of a real moon rock collected at the Sea of Tranquility during the 1969 Apollo 11 mission, the first time humans walked on the moon. Find the dotted line that traces Apollo 11's path from Earth to the Moon and back.

The *Space Window* is part of seven stained glass windows that honor different professions. Its official name is the *Scientists and Technicians Window.* Unlike the nearby windows that honor writers, doctors, and others, the *Space Window* doesn't feature any people. It was dedicated in 1974 on the fifth anniversary of the lunar landing. Apollo 11 astronauts Buzz Aldrin, Neil Armstrong, and Michael Collins were at the dedication ceremony!

There's a lot more to explore inside the National Cathedral. The Children's Chapel is kid-sized, with a small organ and chairs, and the walls and chairs are covered with pictures of animals. Nearby is the world's largest cathedral made with LEGO bricks. And the old baptistery outside is now a café called Open City – they serve ice cream.

The cathedral's exterior is covered with 1,242 grotesques, including over 100 gargoyles. Bring binoculars and look for a rattlesnake, donkey, and elephant – and even Darth Vader!

Address 3101 Wisconsin Avenue NW, Washington, DC 20016, +1 (202) 537-6200, www.cathedral.org, info@cathedral.org // **Getting there** Bus C85, D80, D82 to Wisconsin Avenue & Woodley Road NW // **Hours** See website for updated visitor information // **Ages** 2+

TIP: The Bishop's Garden outside displays beautiful seasonal flowers and plants.

92_STANTON PARK TOYS

Play with community toys

Kid-sized cars, a firetruck, and tractor are all toys you can find at Stanton Park, one of several public parks on Capitol Hill. No, these toys don't belong to a neighborhood kid. They are all community toys, which means they are always at the park's enclosed playground for anyone to ride and enjoy. And neighbors often add to the collection. Just make sure to take turns with other kids while you're there. After riding around in a pink or green car, go down the slide or play tic-tac-toe with a friend using the giant game board.

These toys are all inside Stanton Park, a neighborhood park with a history. When Washington, DC was created with land given by the states of Maryland and Virginia, a Frenchman named Pierre L'Enfant created a plan for the city. L'Enfant's plan included grand avenues and lush parks, and Stanton Park was included in his original plan.

TIP: Nearby Northeast Library has weekly events for infants and toddlers.

Locals have enjoyed this park for well over 150 years. In the center, you'll find a giant statue of Nathanael Greene riding a horse. He was a Revolutionary War hero who served with George Washington. His statue isn't the only nod to American history. Stanton Park itself is named after Edwin M. Stanton, President Abraham Lincoln's Secretary of War. He helped the Union win the Civil War, ending slavery in the country.

happy

Stanton Park is also one of the most popular places for locals to find DC's famous cherry trees every spring. Branches filled with pink blossoms hang over the park's paths and benches. It's a sight to see!

Address 226 4th Street NE, Washington, DC 20002, +1 (771) 208-1453, www.nps.gov/cahi/learn/historyculture/cahi_stanton.htm // **Getting there** Metro to Union Station (Red Line) // **Hours** Unrestricted // **Ages** 2+

93_SYCAMORE & OAK

Shop at a community hub

Everything you want is under one roof at Sycamore & Oak, the beautiful retail village on the old campus of Saint Elizabeths Hospital in Congress Heights.

If you love flowers, visit local artist Chris Pyrate's store here for shoes and shirts painted with pink flowers. Forget the tourist hats sold along the National Mall – pick up a cool, local hat instead at The Museum or ask to see its colorful pairs of sneakers made in collaboration with NBA basketball star Steph Curry. The store Paradyce sells puzzles of its logo – a yellow globe where each continent is a different color.

If you're hungry, find Glizzys and order a "glizzy," which is what DC natives call hot dogs. Glizzys' hot dogs are made with vegetables only, but you wouldn't know it. The "Capitol Hill Carrot Dog" is made with carrots and tastes better than meat!

Sycamore & Oak is more than a retail village. It's a model of how to develop an area where neighbors take the lead. It hosts Black-owned businesses, including entrepreneurs from the Congress Heights community. The impressive wood structure is designed by David Adjaye, the same architect behind the National African American History & Culture Museum. There are regular events here too, from music to the annual Go-Go Santa, a free event featuring a Black Santa. Sycamore & Oak is also a place where kids can run around the enclosed, state-of-the-art playground with three play areas, including a massive ropes course. There's plenty of seating across two levels.

Address 1110 Oak Drive SE, Washington, DC 20032, www.sycamoreandoak.com // **Getting there** Metro to Congress Heights (Green Line) // **Hours** Tue–Thu 11am–7pm, Fri & Sat 10am–8pm, Sun noon–5pm // **Ages** 2+

TIP: More than 200 cherry trees bloom every spring at nearby Oxon Run Park.

94_TIDAL BASIN PEDAL BOATS

See famous monuments on water

There's only one place you can rent pedal boats in Washington, DC, and that's at the Tidal Basin, the perfect place to spend time on the water. Many people know the Tidal Basin as the home of famous memorials, but it's also home to many interesting facts. For example, until 1925 there used to be a beach for swimming. There was even a diving platform in the middle of the water. Another fun tidbit to know is that 250 million gallons of water from the Potomac River enter through the inlet gates twice a day at high tide, according to the National Park Service website. That's so much water! It's like taking 25,000 baths.

Today, an array of sights can be seen from the water. You'll see the National Mall's newest addition, the Martin Luther King Jr. Memorial. The giant statue of the civil rights leader gazes directly across the water at the Thomas Jefferson Memorial, where you'll spot the bronze statue of the third US president looking towards The White House. The presidential house may be hard to see from here, but you can't miss the Washington Monument, which was the world's tallest structure when it was dedicated in 1885.

TIP: Learn about the Holocaust through the eyes of a child at the "Daniel's Story" exhibit in the United States Holocaust Memorial Museum.

If you can, rent pedal boats during cherry blossom season. During peak season, usually at the end of March or early April, the famous cherry blossoms paint the Tidal Basin in pink. Cherry trees, 3,020 in total, were given to the US by Japan in 1912 as an act of friendship. Some original trees remain, and others joined over the years. Cherry blossom season is the most beautiful time in DC.

Address 1501 Maine Avenue SW, Washington, DC 20024, +1 (202) 479-2426, www.boatingindc.com/tidal-basin // **Getting there** Metro to Smithsonian (Blue, Orange, Silver Lines) // **Hours** Pedal Boats: Mar–Oct Mon–Fri 9am–6pm, Sat & Sun 10am–6pm; Tidal Basin: unrestricted // **Ages** 4+

95_THE TITANIC MEMORIAL

A statue that inspired a famous movie

One of the most popular movies of all time is *Titanic* (1997), a love story set on the "unsinkable" ship that actually sank in 1912. There's a scene in the movie where the main characters, Rose and Jack, stretch out their arms while standing at the bow of the ship, as if they're flying over the icy Atlantic Ocean. That scene was inspired by the *Titanic* Memorial here in DC.

There weren't enough lifeboats to save everyone on the ship. Many men gave their lives to help save women and children. Shortly after the disaster, a group of women survivors started raising money to build a memorial honoring the men who were lost. Nineteen years later, the *Titanic* Memorial was dedicated, funded and designed by women. Then First Lady Lou Henry Hoover and former First Lady Helen Herron Taft attended the dedication ceremony.

The *Titanic* Memorial was originally in another part of town before it was placed along the Washington Channel in the Southwest Waterfront. A towering statue connects to a granite bench, a perfect place to read a book or rest for a while. It's fun to watch passing boats along the water.

A touching, DC tradition happens here, too. Every April 15, at half past midnight, around the time the HMS *Titanic* struck an iceberg, the Men's Titanic Society gathers to lay wreaths and raise a toast in honor of the men who sacrificed their lives. The event follows a 10pm dinner at the National Press Club, where the menu mimics the last meal served on the *Titanic* before it sank down to the ocean's floor.

Address Southwest Waterfront Park, near P & 14th Street SW, Washington, DC 20005, www.nps.gov/nama/planyourvisit/titanic.htm // Getting there Metro to Waterfront (Green & Yellow Lines) // Hours Unrestricted // Ages 2+

TIP: Close by is Wheat Row, 18th-century houses that are among the city's oldest.

96_TIVOLI'S ASTOUNDING MAGIC

Find hidden games in a magic shop

Tivoli's Astounding Magic Supply Company is the only magic store in DC, and it's fun. Pick up a pencil case that makes pencils disappear. "Dizzy Dice" change colors every time you roll them. You can buy a coloring book that reveals a blank, colored, or black-and-white outline page depending on how you open it. A favorite trick is the "Flying Butterfly," a paper butterfly with a twisted rubber band inside a book that flies out when the book is opened. Everything in the shop is kid-approved and kid-friendly. If you're gentle, you can play with anything in the store.

The tricks and toys are only half the fun. Throughout the store are hidden messages or items, some that only kids find. For example, handwriting on a mirror may look like gibberish, but to kids, it reads "You are outstanding." Look hard, and you may stumble upon a picture of a dog in a top hat.

Games are hidden throughout the store too. If you find the cannon and throw a playing card inside, you get a discount. There's a giant gumball machine that spits out fortunes written by kids. (If you don't have the 25 cents for the machine, the staff will give you a quarter.)

Make sure you explore the entire store. The highlight is a secret door that leads to a workshop space. This is where 826, the country's largest youth writing network, hosts creative writing sessions for kids ages 6 to 18 years old. Learn how to express yourself through writing. All the kids get their books published and placed into select DC Public Libraries.

Address 3333 14th Street NW, Washington, DC 20010, +1 (202) 417-6109, www.astoundingmagic.com, magic@826dc.org // Getting there Metro to Columbia Heights (Green & Yellow Lines) // Hours Sat 11am–4pm // Ages 2+

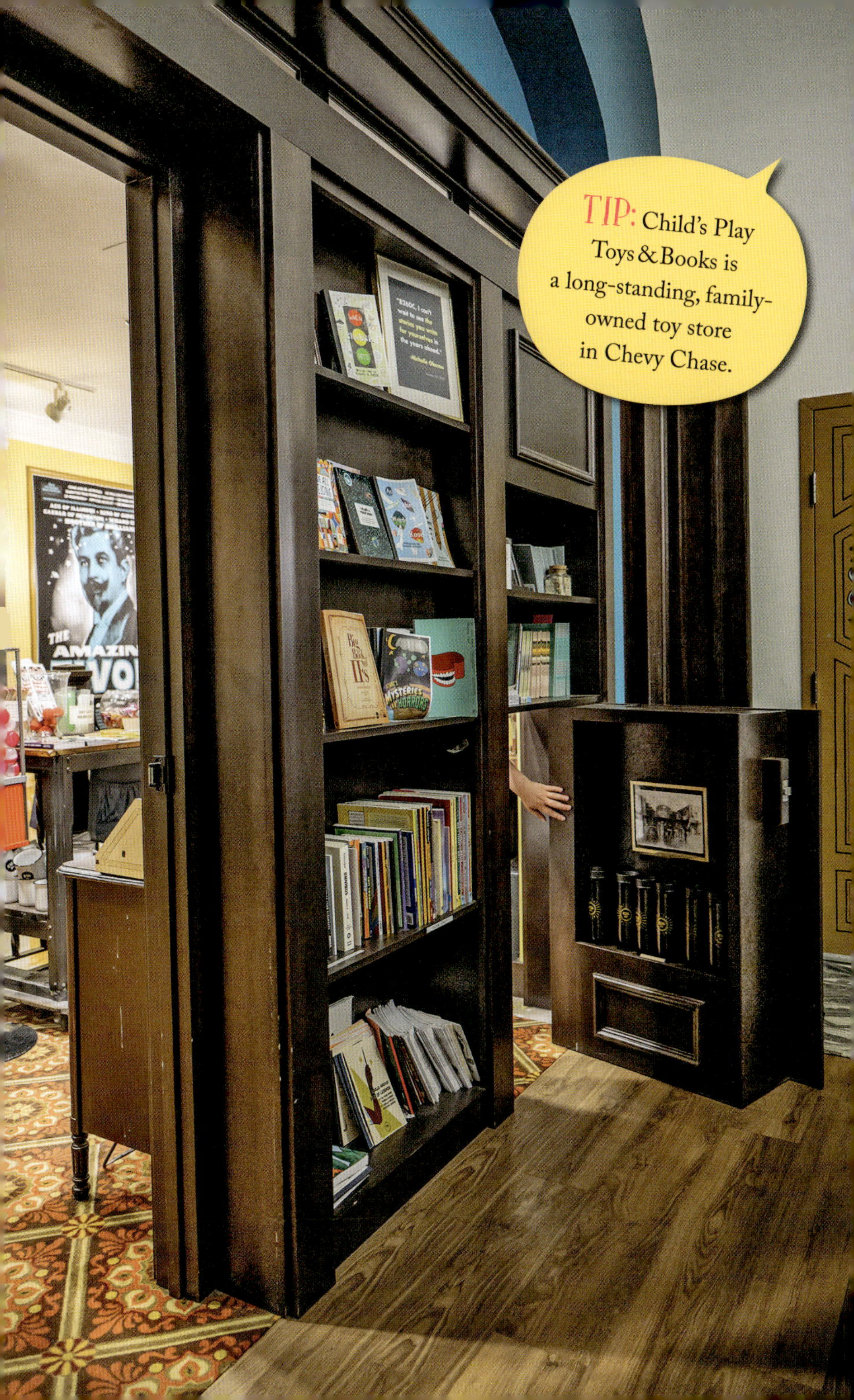

TIP: Child's Play Toys & Books is a long-standing, family-owned toy store in Chevy Chase.

97_TOTEM POLES FOR 9/11

Indigenous Americans in the capital

It's surprising to see giant totem poles inside historic Congressional Cemetery, and there is indeed a story behind them. After the September 11, 2001 terrorist attacks, the Lummi Nation, Indigenous Americans who live in what's now Washington State, wanted to help the country heal. A Lummi master carver named Jewel Praying Wolf James made totem poles for each site affected by the attacks. The Pentagon didn't have space for the totem poles, so they were placed in Congressional Cemetery along the 9/11 Memorial Path there.

One of the poles is called Liberty and the other Freedom. There are many symbols carved into them. Look for the mother and father bears representing the Moon and Sun. The eagles on each pole depict War and Peace, and each eagle has seven feathers. That's to honor the American Airlines Flight 77 that crashed into The Pentagon on September 11. The totem poles are also reminders of the Indigenous land on which they stand. Before Europeans came to what's now DC, the Nacotchtank and the Piscataway peoples lived here.

There's more to explore at Congressional Cemetery, which was created in 1807. A US Vice President, many US politicians, and 70,000 others rest here. At the cemetery's entrance is a wooden box with guides. One points you to the 36 Indigenous people buried here, many of whom came to DC to advocate for their people. Find the gravestone of Kan Ya Tu Duta, or Scarlet Crow, of the Sisseton Wahpeton Sioux tribe, from what's now North and South Dakota.

Address 1801 E Street SE, Washington, DC 20003, on Prout Street between Sections 4&7, +1 (202) 543-0539, www.congressionalcemetery.org // Getting there Metro to Potomac Avenue (Blue, Orange, Silver Lines) // Hours Daily dawn–dusk // Ages 2+

TIP: Nearby is The Roost, a food hall with a kids menu and arcade games.

98_ *TRANSFORMERS* STATUES

Bumblebee and Optimus Prime made from car parts

If you're a fan of *Transformers*, then wander to Georgetown, one of DC's fanciest neighborhoods. Among historic rowhouses and mansions are giant *Transformers* statues. Even if you're not a fan, you'll still recognize the famous cars that turn into machines and battle it out in their movies. Reaching almost ten feet tall, two statues guard the front door of the home of Dr. Howard Newton, a scientist and Georgetown University professor. Bumblebee is the yellow one, and Optimus Prime is blue. Both weigh two tons and are made from motorcycle and car parts. Notice the figures' feet – they are made from old wheel rims. How many rims can you count?

People come from far and wide to snap a photo with the *Transformers* statues, but their presence has a deeper meaning. Dr. Newton's work focuses on artificial intelligence. He believes in the power of machines and inventions to help humankind. His message is that machines and humans can live in harmony. After all, the *Transformers* statues honor the movie machines that come from another planet to save Earth. That's why Dr. Newton commissioned an artist in Taiwan to create the statues for all to enjoy as they walk by.

A collector of cars, Dr. Newton also displays many car parts, robots, and additional *Transformers* statues inside his home. You can't walk inside, but if you look up, you'll notice even more *Transformers* on his rooftop, guarding Georgetown. It's a quirky addition to a posh neighborhood, but one welcomed by kids everywhere.

TIP: Nearby is the memorial to Francis Scott Key, who wrote the National Anthem.

Address 3614 Prospect Street NW, Washington, DC 20007 // **Getting there** Bus C91 to Prospect & 36th Streets NW // **Hours** Unrestricted // **Ages** 2+

3614

99_TRANSPORTATION WALK

Climb on a dump truck tire

Ah

The Transportation Walk breaks all the museum rules. First of all, you don't need a ticket. Secondly, it's open all day and night. It never closes. Whenever you want to visit, you just show up. Finally, you can climb on its artifacts. Spread out along four blocks wrapping around the US Department of Transportation in the Navy Yard neighborhood are wheels, propellers, tires, and more. A dump truck tire? You can climb it. Locate a ship's helm and try steering it. The Transportation Walk is extremely interactive.

Oh

This outdoor museum screams fun, but you'll learn a thing or two as well. The Transportation Walk is organized around four themes: Encounter and Exploration, Industry and Expansion, Greater Mobility, and Modern Era. Each theme talks about how transportation has evolved from 1600 to today. Find the sculpture honoring Edward Converse, the country's first ferryman, who transported passengers across Boston's Charles River in 1631. Three wooden wheels tell the story of how covered wagons carried opportunists during the California Gold Rush. Read how many seconds Orville Wright's first airplane flew for. Touch an airplane wheel and learn how the Airline Deregulation Act made flying more accessible to all people in 1978.

While you're touching a ship's propeller or climbing a railroad crossing sign, don't miss learning about famous people like Amelia Earhart, the first woman and second person to make the solo flight across the Atlantic Ocean, or Sally Ride, the first American woman in space.

Address 100 Tingey Street SE, Washington, DC 20003, +1 (202) 366-4000, www.capitolriverfront.org/go/walking-museum-of-transportation // **Getting there** Metro to Navy Yard–Ballpark (Green & Yellow Lines) // **Hours** Unrestricted // **Ages** 2+

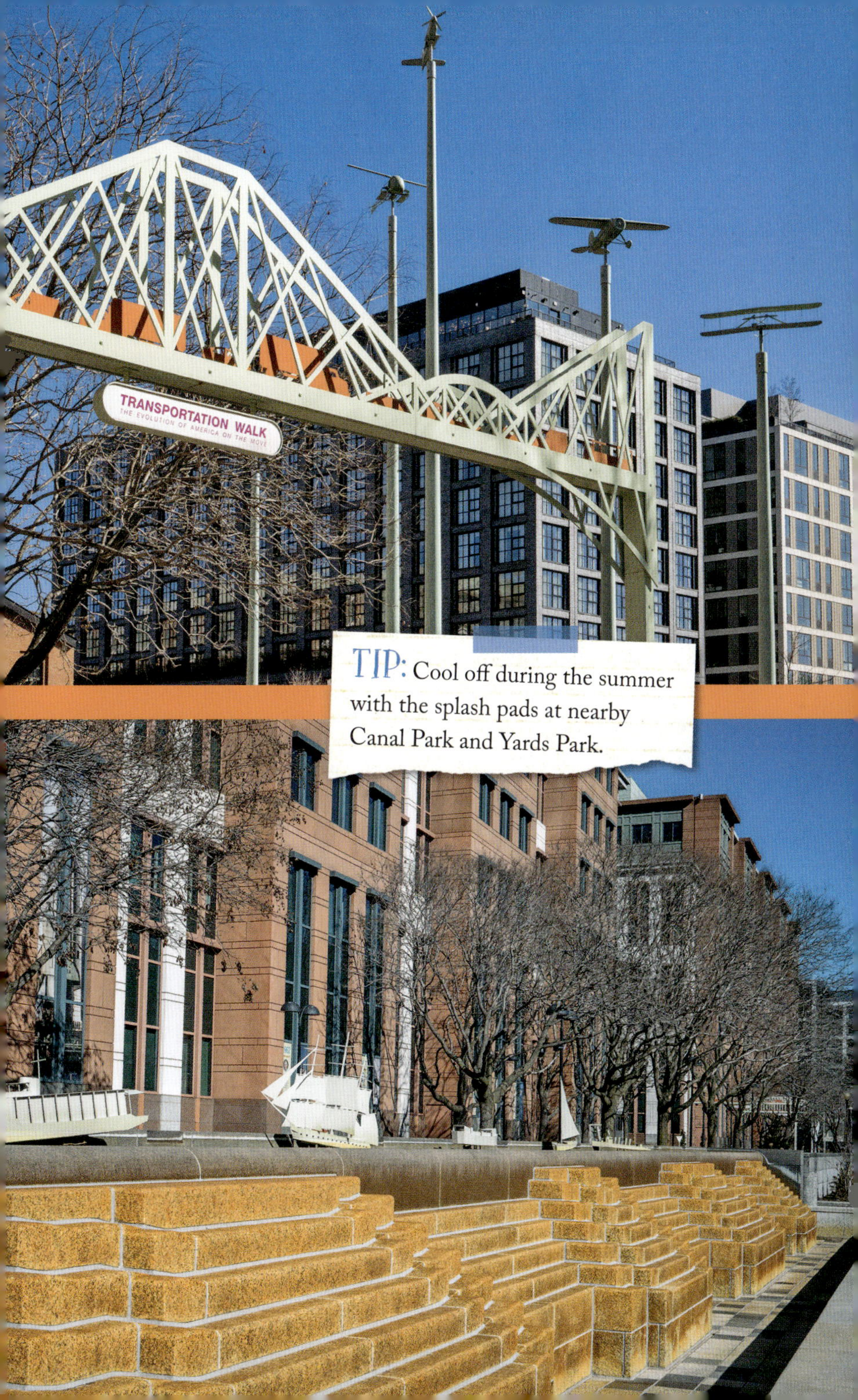

TIP: Cool off during the summer with the splash pads at nearby Canal Park and Yards Park.

100_TREGARON CONSERVANCY

A hidden forest where frogs live

What's the difference between a bullfrog and a toad? Bullfrogs usually have wet, smooth skin, while toads typically have dry, bumpy skin. You'll learn that fact and more at Tregaron Conservancy, a hidden forest in Cleveland Park, where you can follow trails to a lily pond that's home to goldfish, ducks, and frogs. Along the way, you may spot sparrows, woodpeckers, hawks, and over 130 more species of birds.

Far from the hustle and bustle of Downtown DC, Tregaron Conservancy used to be the estate of several wealthy people, including Marjorie Merriweather Post, the heiress to a cereal company and the wealthiest woman in the country. Ellen Biddle Shipman, one of the first women landscape architects in the country, designed its gardens, which you can still see today.

No matter when you go, you'll find flowers in all colors and shades. April brings daffodils, May pink dogwoods, and June hydrangeas. Many of the flowers found here are native to DC. The plants that aren't native are generally removed, as they threaten to take over native plants.

In addition to finding wildlife and learning about native organisms like turkey tail fungi, there's a lot more to do inside Tregaron Conservancy. Pick up a map at each entrance and learn how to read it to find your way. A fallen tree makes for a natural playground when you can climb on it! Throughout the year, there's story time and performances. Every April, it hosts one of the city's largest Easter egg hunts, hiding around 3,500 plastic eggs with goodies inside.

Address 3100 Macomb Street Northwest, Washington, DC 20008, +1 (202) 810-5009, www.tregaron.org // **Getting there** Metro to Cleveland Park (Red Line) // **Hours** Daily dawn–dusk // **Ages** 0+

TIP: Eat Japanese-inspired pastries in a hidden courtyard at nearby SakuSaku Flakerie.

101_UNICORN STATUES

Marvel at these mystical creatures

If you're looking for unicorns, you won't find them at the National Zoo. The only unicorns you'll find in DC guard a small townhouse community. On the sides of the gate to Chatsworth Townhomes are two giant unicorn statues. They're not out of place. The road that wraps around Chatsworth is called Unicorn Lane, and the two unicorn statues look straight out of a fairytale.

Even for locals, the unicorn statues are a mystery, but, like everything in DC, they tell a story. The land Chatsworth is on used to be the estate of a woman named Emma T. Hahm, who ran a restaurant in the city. After she passed away in 1949, the land sat unused until the Soviet Union decided to build its embassy here at the height of the Cold War. Neighbors protested. The Soviet Union built its embassy elsewhere.

Years later, a developer took control of the land to build a gated community. The project needed a road, which had to match the pattern of the nearby East/West streets, a three-syllable word in between Tennyson and Worthington Streets NW. There aren't many "U" words with three syllables. "Underwear" and "urinal" weren't very good options. But "Unicorn" was perfect, and thus Unicorn Lane was born, according to The Hill Is Home website.

The unicorns along Unicorn Lane are the symbol of Chatsworth. They stand at the community's entrance, where residents pass daily. A few famous people have lived at Chatsworth, such as Ron Brown, the US Secretary of Commerce under President Bill Clinton, who definitely saw the unicorns!

TIP: Feel like you're escaping the city while you hike the nearby Rock Creek Trail.

Address Unicorn Lane & Oregon Avenue NW, Washington, DC 20015 // **Getting there** Bus C83 to Oregon Avenue & Unicorn Lane NW // **Hours** Unrestricted // **Ages** 1+

102_US CAPITOL TREES

Learn about history through trees

Every tree has a story, especially those around the US Capitol. Surrounding the iconic building are around 4,800 trees from all 50 states and the territories, different countries, and some very special trees too. Find the Space Tree, a sweetgum tree from a seed that went into space on NASA's Artemis I mission in 2022. Learn about First Lady Claudia Alta "Lady Bird" Johnson, who planted a Chinese dogwood here. She's known and loved for planting wildflowers along the country's highways. The Liberty Tree here was grown using a sapling from a tree at Independence Hall in Philadelphia.

You probably know that DC gets very hot during the summer. Before air conditioning was invented, the US Capitol's landscape architect Frederick Law Olmsted planted trees to provide shade. Forty-five of his original trees remain. Olmsted's Summer House remains on the National Mall side of the Capitol near Constitution Avenue NW, where you can sip from an old drinking fountain.

Most of the trees here have plaques that share the species and history. For example, on the side of the Capitol facing the Washington Monument is the Anne Frank Tree, which was taken from a sapling of the original horse chestnut tree at her residence in Amsterdam. Visit it and honor the Jewish girl who wrote in her diary while in hiding during the Holocaust.

The US Capitol grounds happen to be one of the country's largest arboretums, a botanical garden of trees and shrubs. You are free to explore the grounds, picnic on the grass, and get close to the trees.

Address US Capitol, Washington, DC 20515, +1 (202) 226-8000, www.aoc.gov/explore-capitol-campus/features/trees // **Getting there** Metro to Capitol South (Blue, Orange, Silver Lines) // **Hours** Unrestricted // **Ages** 2+

TIP: Find more trees, including cherry blossoms, at nearby Lower Senate Park.

103_WANGARI GARDENS

A community garden tribute to a Nobel laureate

The first African woman to win the Nobel Peace Prize was Wangari Maathai in 2004 for leading the Green Belt Movement, which inspires thousands of women to plant trees across Africa. During her lifetime, Maathai deeply cared about the Earth. A little piece of her legacy lives on, far from her native Kenya, in DC's Park View neighborhood, thanks to a group of neighbors who are inspired by her life.

Wangari Gardens, one of the largest community gardens in the city, is full of herbs, vegetables, fruit, flowers, and more. It's surrounded by roads, but it's easy to escape the city here. The garden is organic, and neighbors have their own plots within a fence. Anything outside of the fence is for the community to enjoy, including a large herb garden. Basil and mint are just two herbs grown here, and they both smell and taste delicious. Go ahead and pull off a leaf to taste them.

There's a public orchard that grows all kinds of fruit, including apples, pears, persimmon, and pawpaw. The pawpaw is native to Washington, DC and tastes like a blend of bananas and mangos. It's used in ice cream, bread, and other yummy recipes.

Wangari Gardens is a place for the people. The 2.5 acres of green space are perfect for a sunset picnic. Regular events are hosted, like a seed-swapping party, garden yoga, foraging and herb workshops, and even an annual fall potluck with a costume party for kids and pumpkin smashing. Yes, you read that right. You can smash pumpkins and not get in trouble!

Address Between Kenyon Street, Park Place, and Irving Street NW, Washington, DC 20010, +1 (202) 670-5459, www.wangarigardens.wordpress.com, wangarigardens@gmail.com // **Getting there** Metro to Columbia Heights (Green & Yellow Lines) // **Hours** Unrestricted // **Ages** 0+

TIP: Try the Ethiopian breakfast at nearby Heat Da Spot Café.

104_ WASHINGTON MONUMENT

An elevator ride to remember

The best way to see the Washington Monument, DC's famously tall tower, is from the top. If you're lucky enough to snag free but limited tickets, a National Park Service ranger will take you to the top in a small, historic elevator, and the ride is part of the fun.

When the Washington Monument opened in 1888 to honor the first President of the United States, its elevator was only used to carry stone. The ride to the top took 10 minutes! Fortunately, the current elevator is modern and only takes 70 seconds to travel 555 feet into the air. And you won't feel a pit in your stomach like you do on roller coasters, as the Washington Monument's elevator offers a smooth ride.

At the top, you'll find small windows with epic views of DC. From one side, you'll see the US Capitol. From another, you'll find the Tidal Basin. One floor below is an exhibit about the monument, where you'll learn the answers to questions like "Why is the Washington Monument two different colors?" The answer is because they stopped construction during the Civil War and later used stone from a different quarry to finish it.

Take your time enjoying the views, and then take the elevator back down to the ground. The original elevator had seats for guests. The new one doesn't, but the ride down is magical. Halfway through, it slows down for you to see commemorative stones from different states. There's jade from Alaska and petrified wood from Arizona. If you're from the United States, look for your state's stone!

TIP: Visit the Memorial to the 56 Signers of the Declaration of Independence in Constitution Gardens.

Address 2 15th Street NW, Washington, DC, +1 (202) 426-6841, www.nps.gov/wamo/index.htm // Getting there Metro to Smithsonian (Blue, Orange, Silver Lines) // Hours Daily 9am–5pm // Ages 0+

105_ WATERGATE STEPS

Run up and down grand steps

When most people hear the word "Watergate," they think of the famous presidential scandal from the 1970s that took place in the Watergate building complex in DC. But the original Watergate is actually 40 grand steps built in 1932 right behind the Lincoln Memorial. These steps were built to serve as a dock, where boats would drop off important people, including politicians and celebrities, who'd then walk up the steps to go see the Lincoln Memorial.

It didn't turn out like that. Instead, the famous steps were used for concerts. For 30 years, bands and musicians played on boats anchored in the Potomac River to large crowds sitting on the steps. With the sunset as a backdrop, it was a beautiful venue. Then the noise from planes landing at the nearby airport got too loud, and the concerts ended.

Today, the steps aren't used for anything official. In fact, some think they lead to nowhere. It's a valid thought, as the steps simply lead to a sidewalk along the Potomac River. However, locals keep the steps alive. Joggers run up and down them for exercise. Friends often gather on the steps with a picnic to watch the sun setting over Rosslyn, a neighborhood in Arlington, Virginia across the river.

If you need a place to let out lots of energy, you can race up and down the Watergate Steps, and enjoy the river view. Don't miss the giant horse and Pegasus (a horse with wings) statues on either side of the Watergate Steps. And then head up the steps to visit the Lincoln Memorial.

Address Ohio Drive SW, Washington, DC 20004 // **Getting there** Metro to Foggy Bottom-GWU (Blue, Orange, Silver Lines) // **Hours** Unrestricted // **Ages** 2+

TIP: Watch an exciting game of volleyball at the Parkway Drive Volleyball Courts.

106_WATERMELON HOUSE

Don't eat this watermelon

How a huge mural of a watermelon appeared on the side of a 19th-century rowhouse in Shaw is a funny story. When Wade Sterk and his partner moved into the small rowhouse, it was painted a mint green. Being along an alley, the side of the house often got tagged with graffiti, which wasn't nice. For his partner's birthday, Sterk decided to paint the house a new color – pink! But when he opened the paint can, he realized the pink looked like Pepto-Bismol.

So he decided to turn lemons into lemonade. Well, watermelon lemonade. Despite having no formal art training, he painted the watermelon mural on the side of his house. Of course, it drew the attention of neighbors. Some loved it, others did not. A few years on, it's now a beloved part of the community.

People travel from across the region to snap photos in front of the famous mural. So many people visited that Sterk decided to add a kiwi and pineapple mural near the watermelon. By the pineapple mural are the words, "Stand tall, wear a crown, and be sweet inside." It inspires all who visit, and that's Sterk's goal. He wants the murals to bring laughter and spread joy.

Sterk is always finding ways to add murals nearby. Recruiting neighbor and artist McLane Harrington, Sterk had a mural of a fruit cup and famous places in DC added close by, in which you'll find handprints from community members – schoolchildren, churchgoers, and even paw prints from furry friends. There are "Easter eggs" for you to find, too, including a hidden rat.

Address 1112 Q Street NW, Washington, DC 20009, +1 (202) 910-7130, www.watermelonhouse.com, wadesterk@watermelonhouse.com // **Getting there** Metro to Shaw-Howard University (Green & Yellow Lines) // **Hours** Unrestricted, viewable from the outside only // **Ages** 1+

TIP: Find Lisa Marie Thalhammer's rainbow-painted LOVE mural in nearby Blagden Alley.

107 _ WEGMANS WONDERPLACE

Play in a famous chef's kitchen at the NMAH

You can pretend to be a chef in the kid-sized kitchen at the National Museum of American History's (NMAH) Wegmans Wonderplace, the first exhibit space along the National Mall designed for kids. Imagine you're cooking omelets, serving your yummy creation to family at the breakfast bar. The kitchen in which you're standing is modeled after a very famous chef named Julia Child. She was one of the first chefs on television to teach people how to cook. She was also a spy during World War II!

Once you're done cooking in the kitchen, go on your own spy quest to find animals hidden throughout Wegmans Wonderplace. Among plastic vegetables and fruit, like potatoes and oranges at The Farm, is a statue of a chicken and a cow. Crawl up the tower called The Climber, and spot more chickens. You may need to look high in the sky to find more.

Finish spotting most of the animals, and then go see the famous collections throughout Wegmans Wonderplace. There's a portrait gallery featuring kids. Can you find the collections of spoons and Hot Wheels? While you search, reflect on what collection you may start. After all, the space you're in is one of many museums in DC that feature famous collections.

TIP: See giant dinosaur bones at the Smithsonian National Museum of Natural History next door.

If you've outgrown Wegmans Wonderplace, the Spark! Lab is next door, where you can pretend to be an inventor. Create your own city block or lay out a pinball course with real flippers and the works. Test out your invention to make sure it works. If it doesn't, use your imagination to recreate the pinball course.

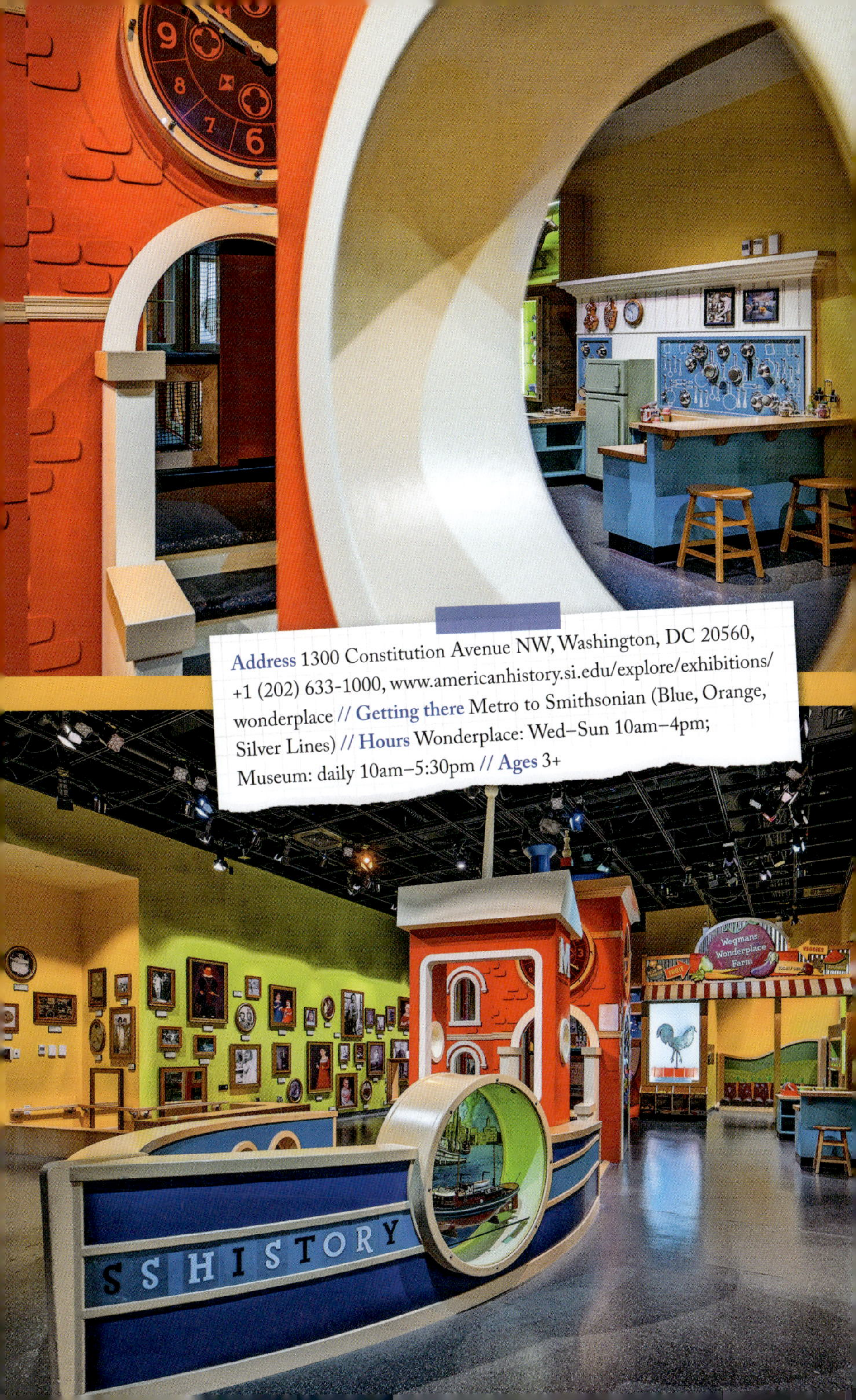

Address 1300 Constitution Avenue NW, Washington, DC 20560, +1 (202) 633-1000, www.americanhistory.si.edu/explore/exhibitions/wonderplace // **Getting there** Metro to Smithsonian (Blue, Orange, Silver Lines) // **Hours** Wonderplace: Wed–Sun 10am–4pm; Museum: daily 10am–5:30pm // **Ages** 3+

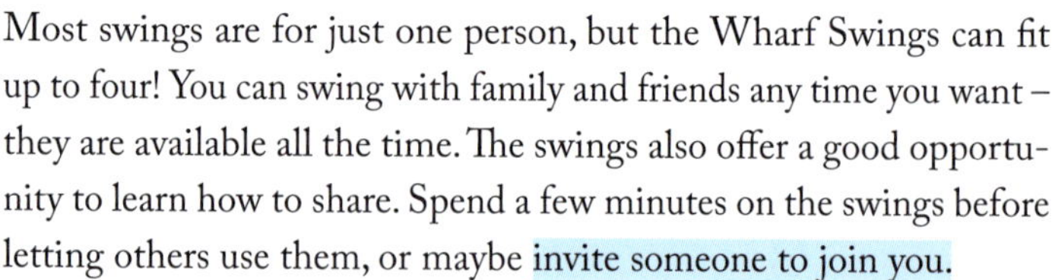

108_WHARF SWINGS

Ride a swing fit for the whole family

Most swings are for just one person, but the Wharf Swings can fit up to four! You can swing with family and friends any time you want – they are available all the time. The swings also offer a good opportunity to learn how to share. Spend a few minutes on the swings before letting others use them, or maybe invite someone to join you.

Along the Washington Channel with views of the Washington Monument, the Wharf Swings sit along Recreation Pier. Surrounded by an area with over 80 shops and restaurants, the Recreation Pier is designed to draw people to the water. It's also a wonderland for kids.

Not only does it have five giant swings, but the floating dock has a fire pit that's lit most hours in the day and night. During the winter months, it's a nice place to warm up. The Recreation Pier is designed to curve, creating little hills for kids to climb on. As you walk the curves, they get narrower the further down the pier you go. How long can you walk until it's too steep?

The Recreation Pier and the swings are part of The Wharf, an area along the water that was developed in 2017. You'll find many restaurants for all ages, including several places to grab ice cream. Near the Recreation Pier is a popular splash pad. During the winter, one of the nearby piers turns into a floating ice skating rink. Close by is a trailer that sells kits for making your own s'mores, which you can make and eat by a bonfire. If music is your thing, there are two music halls that host events for kids.

Address 1001 7th Street SW, Washington, DC 20024, +1 (202) 688-3590, www.wharfdc.com // Getting there Metro to Waterfront (Green Line) // Hours Unrestricted // Ages 0+

TIP: Take a ferry ride on the Potomac from The Wharf to Georgetown or Old Town Alexandria.

109_WOMEN'S SUFFRAGE MURAL

Learn history through color

Did you know that women didn't have the right to vote in the United States of America until 1920? Only certain men could vote in elections. Women couldn't even vote for the president. For many years, women fought for that right until, finally, the 19th Amendment gave them the right to vote. The fight for the right to vote is called Women's Suffrage, and it was led by many women of color who sacrificed a lot for the sake of others.

One of the most powerful murals in DC honors women of color who fought for the right for women to vote. Located in historic Anacostia and dedicated on the 100th anniversary of the 19th Amendment, *A Legacy of Resilience* is a mural featuring three art pieces by three different local artists, all women of color. MISS CHELOVE painted Zitkála-Šá (of the Yankton Sioux tribe) and Mary Church Terrell, a First Nations leader and a Black pioneer activist respectively. They each spent a lot of time in DC fighting for equality. Mia DuVall's *Ain't I A Woman* uses shades of purple to honor the heroism of the suffragists. Candice S. Taylor's mural *Onward and Upward We Go* is a charge for all future activists to take a stand for equality everywhere. As they painted their murals on the side of this brick building, the artists listened to music by women of color.

A Legacy of Resilience is a gift to the women who fought for the right to vote. As you look at these images, think about why it's important to stand up for equality among all people, not just those who look like you.

Address 2027 Martin Luther King Jr. Avenue SE, Washington DC 20020, www.hmdb.org/m.asp?m=266757 // **Getting there** Metro to Anacostia (Green Line) // **Hours** Unrestricted // **Ages** 2+

TIP: Candice S. Taylor's mural across the street celebrates Black natural hair.

110_YERÉVAN CAFÉ

Travel to Armenia through its food

When people from all around the world come and make DC their home, they often bring their flavors and recipes with them. Yerevan Café is a small café owned by a mom and dad from a country called Armenia in West Asia.

Armenia is one of the oldest countries in the world. You can see some of the world's most beautiful mountains there. There are even extinct volcanoes that haven't erupted for thousands of years. Armenian children play lots of soccer, which they call "football." Another popular sport is chess. All kids have to learn how to play it in school, starting at a very young age.

Armenia is a small country far away from DC, but its food is mighty. Armenian cuisine is known for many different types of food, like *dolma*, which are herbs and rice wrapped in grape leaves, and *lahmajun*, a thin crust topped with minced meat and herbs. People call it "Armenian pizza." Kids especially love the round *gata*, a sweet bread filled with sugar and butter, and the red lentil and apricot soup, since it's a little sweet. The soup comes as a puree and is popular with babies too! Behind Yerevan Café's glass counter are all sorts of cakes, including one with raspberries.

Once you're done eating, stay inside the café and play. Yerevan Café puts out table games, including Connect Four, children's books, toys, and even coloring paper and crayons for all to enjoy. Or order your pastries and sweet treats to go and cross the street to play on the playground at Marie H Reed Recreation Center.

Address 2204 18th Street NW, Washington, DC 20009, +1 (202) 516-5924, www.yerevandc.com, yerevan@yerevandc.com // Getting there Bus C51 or C53 to 18th & California Streets NW // Hours Sun–Thu 10am–8pm, Fri & Sat 10am–9pm // Ages 2+

TIP: Up the road is Sharbat, an Azerbaijani bakery with a popular layered honey cake.

111_ZIPLINE AT BEAUVOIR

Soar through the sky

Few things are more thrilling than a zipline, and one of the only ziplines in Washington, DC is inside Beauvoir Playground on the grounds of the Washington National Cathedral. The zipline has a seat so you can choose how you soar – standing up or sitting down. Younger kids who need a boost can take advantage of a nearby wooden bench closer to the zipline. Stand on the bench, jump on the zipline, and fly. It's a fun ride! The zipline can hold big people too, so adults are welcome to give it a try as well.

After taking turns on the ride, explore the rest of the playground, one of the biggest in DC. It's fully enclosed so that kids have the freedom (and the adults with them have peace of mind) to explore. A popular spot is "Slide Hill," where you'll find slides built for people of all ages. Kids can start small and when they're brave enough, they can try the biggest slide. It's so big that it even goes through the ground before you shoot out the end.

When the playground was being built, teachers and kids were asked for their help in designing it. So you'll find playground favorites, like swings and a large field, but you'll also find little nooks and crannies to explore. The "Log Jam" is a jungle gym of slanted logs that reach 10 feet into the sky. "Treetop Hill" is a maze of tall wooden towers with rope walkways. Find the bear sculpture carved from an old tree that had died and came back to life as art. There are plans underway to make the playground accessible for people of all abilities.

Address 3500 Woodley Road NW, Washington, DC 20016, +1 (202) 537-6485, www.beauvoirschool.org/discover/campus/beauvoir-playground // **Getting there** Bus C51 to Woodley Road & 34th Street NW // **Hours** Mon–Fri 5pm–dusk, Sat & Sun dawn–dusk // **Ages** 2+

TIP: Stop and smell the flowers in the nearby Bishop's Garden.

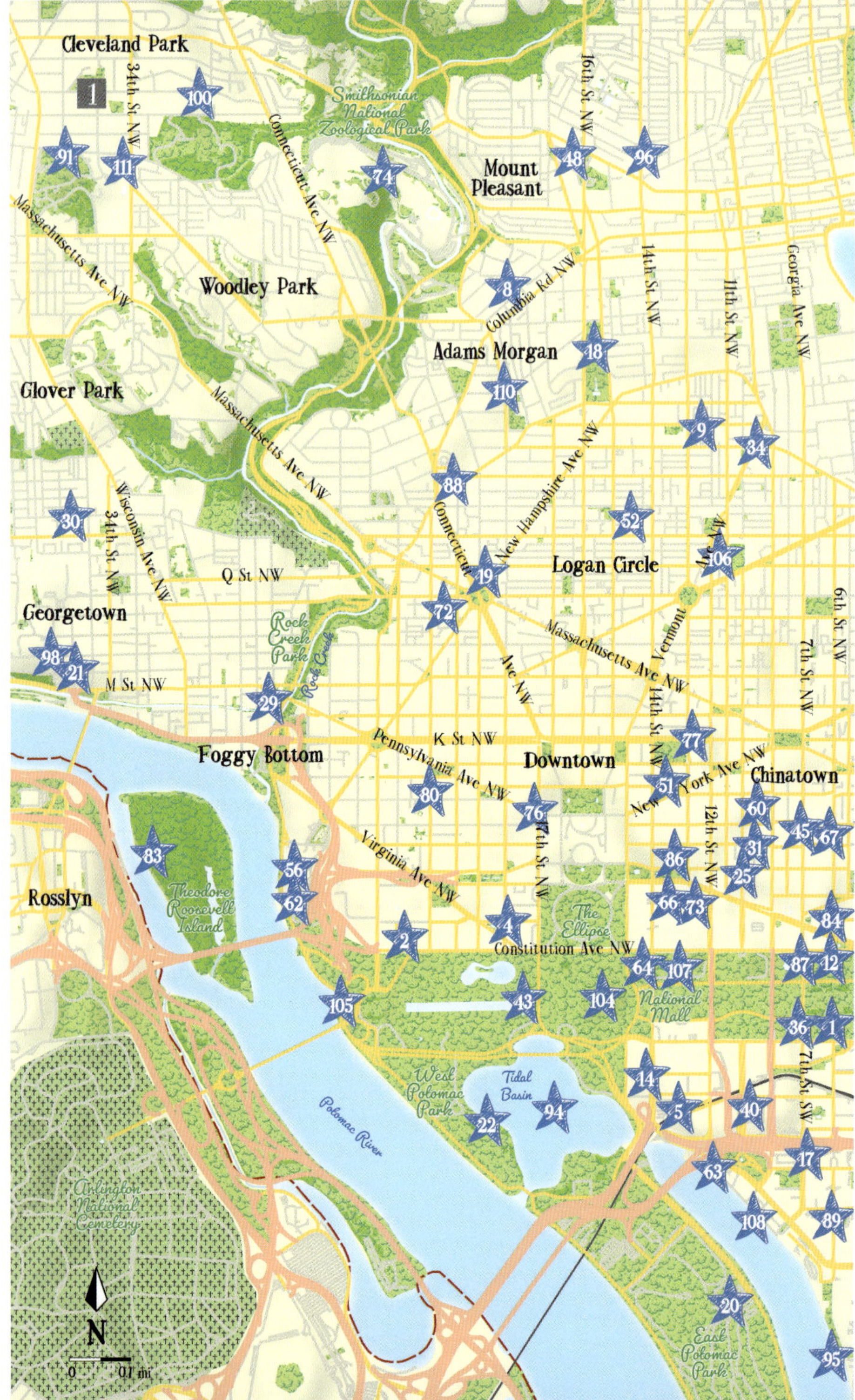

1
Cleveland Park
Woodley Park
Glover Park
Georgetown
Foggy Bottom
Rosslyn
Mount Pleasant
Adams Morgan
Logan Circle
Downtown
Chinatown
Smithsonian National Zoological Park
Rock Creek Park
Theodore Roosevelt Island
The Ellipse
National Mall
West Potomac Park
Tidal Basin
Potomac River
East Potomac Park
Arlington National Cemetery
Connecticut Ave NW
Massachusetts Ave NW
Wisconsin Ave NW
34th St NW
16th St NW
14th St NW
11th St NW
Georgia Ave NW
Columbia Rd NW
New Hampshire Ave NW
Vermont Ave NW
Q St NW
M St NW
K St NW
Pennsylvania Ave NW
New York Ave NW
Virginia Ave NW
17th St NW
12th St NW
7th St NW
6th St NW
Constitution Ave NW
7th St SW
N
0
0.1 mi

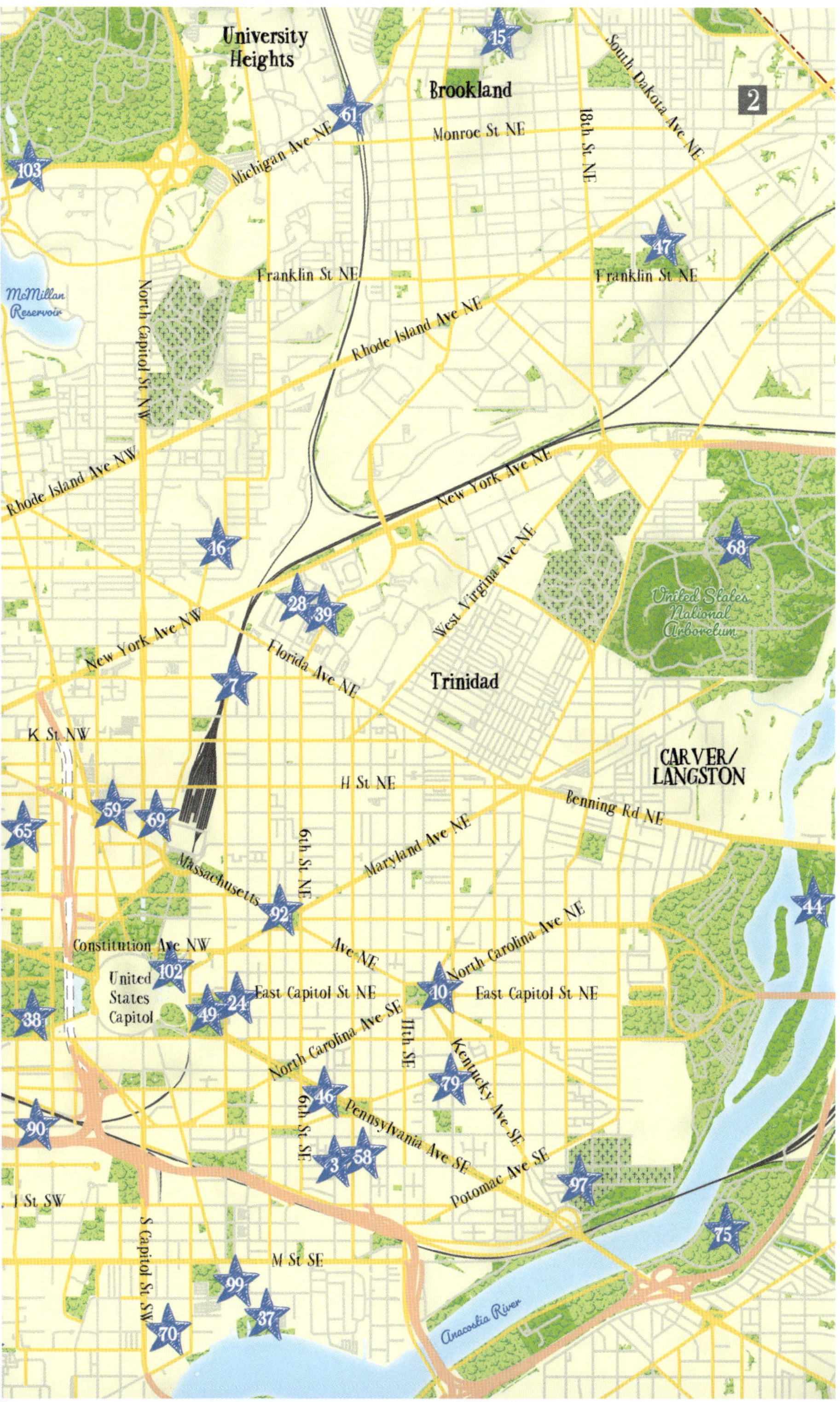
University Heights
Brookland
2
Monroe St NE
Michigan Ave NE
18th St NE
South Dakota Ave NE
McMillan Reservoir
Franklin St NE
Franklin St NE
Rhode Island Ave NE
North Capitol St NW
Rhode Island Ave NW
New York Ave NE
West Virginia Ave NE
United States National Arboretum
New York Ave NW
Florida Ave NE
Trinidad
K St NW
CARVER/ LANGSTON
H St NE
Benning Rd NE
6th St NE
Maryland Ave NE
Massachusetts Ave NE
Constitution Ave NW
United States Capitol
East Capitol St NE
North Carolina Ave NE
East Capitol St NE
North Carolina Ave SE
11th SE
Kentucky Ave SE
6th St SE
Pennsylvania Ave SE
Potomac Ave SE
I St SW
S Capitol St SW
M St SE
Anacostia River
15
61
103
47
16
28
39
68
7
59
69
65
92
44
102
10
24
49
38
46
79
90
3
58
97
75
99
37
70

3
Silver Spring
Adelphi
Langley Park
Bethesda
Shepherd Park
Takoma Park
Lewisdale
Brightwood
Manor Park
Chillum
Friendship Heights
Brightwood Park
Queens Chapel
Fort Totten
American University Park
Michigan Park
Avondale
University Heights
1
Cleveland Park
2
Woodley Park
Glover Park
Arboretum
Bloomingdale
Logan Circle
Georgetown
Trinidad
Langston
Foggy Bottom
Chinatown
Mayfair
Rosslyn
WASHINGTON
Arlington
Capitol Hill
Clarendon
395
695
295
Anacostia
Arlington Heights
Pentagon City
395
Fort Barnard Heights
Potomac River
295
N
0
0.25 mi
101
55
41
57
26
81
82
78
35
71
50
32
23
42
13
53
54
33
109
6
11
27
85
93

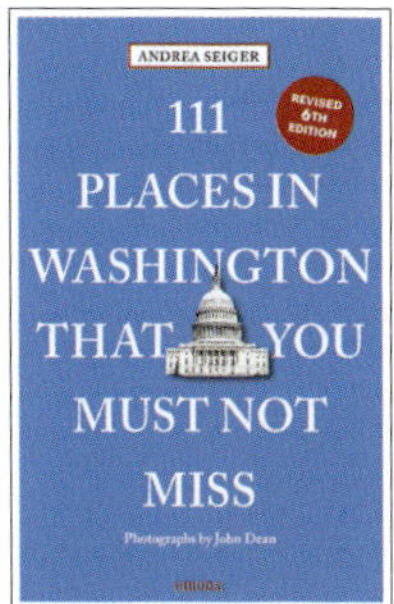

Andrea Seiger, John Dean
111 Places in Washington That You Must Not Miss
ISBN 978-3-7408-2656-7

Paige Muller, Andrea Seiger, Shedrick Pelt
22 Walks in Washington, DC That You Must Not Miss
ISBN 978-3-7408-1987-3

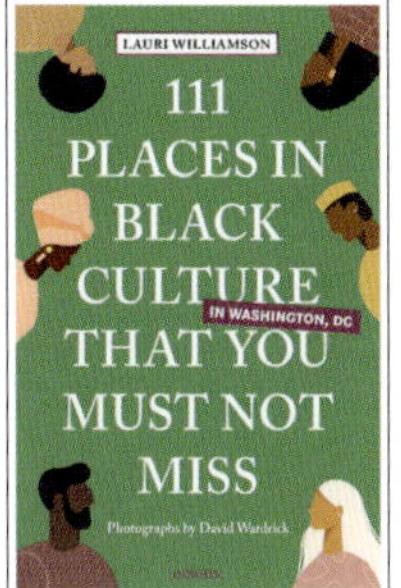

Lauri Williamson, David Wardrick
111 Places in Black Culture in Washington, DC That You Must Not Miss
ISBN 978-3-7408-2003-9

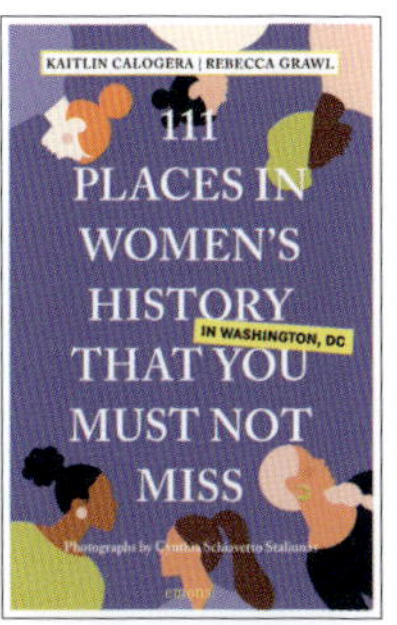

Kaitlin Calogera, Rebecca Grawl, Cynthia Schiavetto Staliunas
111 Places in Women's History in Washington That You Must Not Miss
ISBN 978-3-7408-1590-5

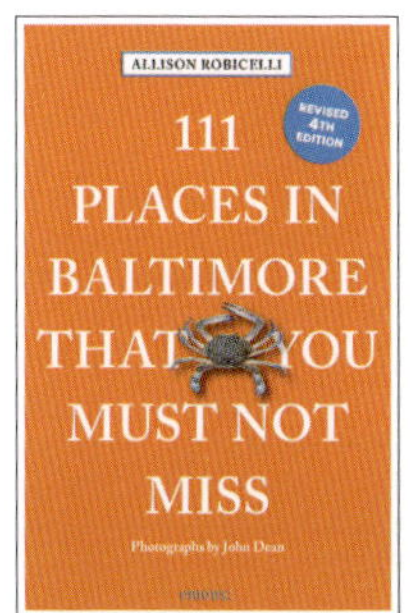

Allison Robicelli, John Dean
111 Places in Baltimore That You Must Not Miss
ISBN 978-3-7408-2571-3

John Tucker, Ashley Tucker
111 Places in Richmond That You Must Not Miss
ISBN 978-3-7408-2653-6

Jo-Anne Elikann, Susan Lusk
111 Places in New York That You Must Not Miss
ISBN 978-3-7408-2400-6

Evan Levy, Rachel Mazor, Jost Heijmenberg
111 Places for Kids in New York That You Must Not Miss
ISBN 978-3-7408-1993-4

Amy Bizzarri, Susie Inverso
111 Places for Kids in Chicago That You Must Not Miss
ISBN 978-3-7408-0599-9

PHOTO CREDITS

All photos by Schiavetto Studios except:
Blue Rooster (ch. 12): Photograph © Board of Trustees, National Gallery of Art, Washington
Catacombs of DC (ch. 15): Photos courtesy of the Franciscan Monastery of the Holy Land in America
Ford's Theatre (ch. 25): Photo by @Schiavetto, Location at Ford's Theatre
Hirshhorn Art School (ch. 36): Storytime Studio. Courtesy of the Hirshhorn Museum and Sculpture Garden, Photo by Rick Coulby
imagiNATIONS (ch. 38): The imagiNATIONS Activity Center in Washington, DC at the National Museum of the American Indian, Photo courtesy of the museum
Musical Crossroads (ch. 68): Photo courtesy of the National Museum of African American History & Culture, Photo by Alan Karchmer
Nationals' Family Fun Day (ch. 70): MLB trademarks used with permission of MLB. All Rights Reserved
Orangutan Crossing (ch. 74): Photo by Jessie Cohen, Smithsonian's National Zoo
The People's House (ch. 76): Photo by Sahar Coston-Hardy / Esto
Saturday Morning Live (ch. 86): Courtesy of The National Theatre Foundation
Sculpture Garden Ice Rink (ch. 87): Photograph © Board of Trustees, National Gallery of Art, Washington

ART CREDITS

Albert Einstein Memorial (ch. 2): Robert Berks
Alphabet Animals (ch. 3): Carolina Mayorga
Blue Rooster (ch. 12): Fritsch, Katharina
Skulptur "Cock / Hahn" (National Gallery of Art/Washington)
© VG Bild-Kunst, Bonn 2025
Fala The Scottish Terrier (ch. 22): Sculpture by Neil Estern
National Fire Dog Monument (ch. 67): Austin Weishel
Plastic Bottle Cap Mural (ch. 78):
Karen A. Lash plastic bottle cap murals
Watermelon House (ch. 106):
The Watermelon House by Wade K. Wilson
Women's Suffrage Mural (ch. 109): MISS CHELOVE,
"Lifting As We Climb: Organizing for Women's Rights,
from Red Bird to the Women's Club Movement," 2020

ACKNOWLEDGEMENTS

There are many people to thank in writing this book. First, Addy. Just a few years old, you showed me a new side to the city. Because of your curiosity, I more deeply know, see, and love Washington, DC. Before Addy, Theresa was and continues to be my exploration partner. The three of us love learning, exploring, and finding the stories that make DC great. I love you both, and our little wandering family. Secondly, there's no book without my editor Karen Seiger. Not only did she help make this book compelling, accessible, and honoring to Washington, DC, but she is a constant source of encouragement and inspiration. Also, thank you to Laura Olk at Emons for getting the book across the finish line.

Cindy Schiavetto, thank you for capturing each place in this book beautifully. Partnering with you was fun and energizing. You helped me see each place with fresh eyes, deepening my appreciation of this city.

Capturing the essence of each place required the help of many people who steward each one. Thank you for your work. Each of you holds the key to some of DC's greatest places. Thank you for your dedication and care. More people know and love this city because of you.

Finally, thank you to every native Washingtonian who told me stories, introduced me to places, and pushed me to explore all parts of Washington, DC. You are the true soul of the city, and no one loves DC more than you.

Austin Graff

I want to express my heartfelt appreciation to the incredible women who have always stood by me – Beth, Jacki, Jeannette, Kristy, Lisa, Mayeluz, Tasha, Tina, and Tracy. Your unwavering support, belief in me, and constant encouragement have made all the difference. May this book spark wonder in both the children you cherish and the child within you, just as photographing it sparked joy in me. Thank you for always being there and for being such a meaningful part of my journey.

Austin, thank you for being such an incredible creative partner throughout this journey – and for walking this path with me. You will always be my "TOASTER!"

Lastly, Adam, Mom, and Dad – thank you for your endless patience and love throughout.

Cynthia Schiavetto Staliunas

Austin K. Graff is a writer, content creator, and social media strategist. After leading social media and influencer marketing teams at International Justice Mission, Coca-Cola Company, and *The Washington Post*, Austin created the first-ever guide to all 131 DC neighborhoods, telling stories of hope throughout the community online.

Cynthia Schiavetto Staliunas is an internationally awarded artist who reveals the strength and beauty within her subjects. A licensed drone pilot, her versatile work spans empowering fine art to dynamic commercial and real estate projects for global clients. Her unique perspective captures both the intimate essence of a person and the grand character of a place.

The information in this book was accurate at the time of publication, but it can change at any time. Please confirm the details for the places you're planning to visit before you head out on your adventures.